P9-DMK-228

More Praise for *First the Jews*

"A short, smart, readable book on a big, ugly, and all-too-timely subject. For a basic introduction to anti-Semitism past and present, the first place to turn is now Rabbi Evan Moffic's *First the Jews*."

—JONATHAN D. SARNA, professor, Brandeis University, and Chief Historian, National Museum of American Jewish History

"Rabbi Moffic has written a book every Christian should read. An essential guide to making sense of the painful history and present reality of anti-Semitism. This is a truly important book."

—ADAM HAMILTON, Senior Pastor, The United Methodist Church of the Resurrection

"Rabbi Moffic's book *First the Jews* is a must-read for those seeking a deeper understanding of the horror of anti-Semitism and its re-emerging reality in America. Rabbi Moffic is an astute observer and so well-grounded in interfaith issues with a great grasp of Roman Catholic tradition."

—REV. JEREMIAH BOLAND, pastor, Archdiocese of Chicago

"There are no shortage of anti-Semitism 'experts' who are eager to denounce it when it comes from one particular side of the political divide. Evan Moffic's latest book is a serious and important contribution in that it unsparingly analyzes all sources of the world's oldest hatred. Moffic's work is particularly incisive and fearless in its treatment of anti-Semitism in the Muslim world—a crucial but sensitive area where many before him have either been silent or trafficked in stereotypes or prejudice. This is an excellent read for any person looking to understand anti-Semitism and to identify ways to combat it."

—DANIEL ELBAUM, Chief Advocacy Officer, American Jewish Committee

"How far the institutional church has strayed from following the rebel-rabbi Jesus! Evan shines light on the need for Christian and Jewish brothers and sisters to come together against this rising tide of hate."

—MICHAEL SLAUGHTER, author, speaker,
pastor emeritus of Ginghamsburg Church

"Rabbi Evan has taught me so much about God, Shalom, and life over the last couple of years. He is incredibly wise, fearless, and always gracious in conversation. And this is why his book, *First the Jews*, is so needed and important. It breaks my heart, but it also invites us to participate in the holy work of peace. Highly recommended."

—AARON NIEQUIST, author of *The Eternal Current: How a Practice-Based Faith Can Save Us from Drowning*

"The old, old subject of anti-Semitism is as current as today's headlines. This emotional and spiritual toxin is a danger to all of humanity, as German Lutheran pastor Martin Niemoeller reminded us in his haunting poem, 'First They Came...', written shortly before he perished in the Holocaust. Rabbi Evan Moffic offers a masterful exploration of contemporary and historical anti-Semitism in this compelling, hopeful book. It is well-researched and worthy of reading and discussion by people of faith everywhere."

—MICHELLE VAN LOON, author of five books including *Born to Wander: Recovering the Value of Our Pilgrim Identity*

FIRST
THE
JEWS

COMBATING THE WORLD'S
LONGEST-RUNNING HATE CAMPAIGN

RABBI EVAN MOFFIC

ABINGDON PRESS
NASHVILLE

FIRST THE JEWS
COMBATING THE WORLD'S LONGEST-RUNNING HATE CAMPAIGN
Copyright © 2019 by Evan Moffic

Library of Congress Cataloging-in-Publication Data

Names: Moffic, Evan, 1978- author.
Title: First the Jews : combating the world's longest-running hate campaign / Evan Moffic.
Description: Nashville : Abingdon Press, [2019] | Includes bibliographical references.
Identifiers: LCCN 2018022202 (print) | LCCN 2018052389 (ebook) | ISBN 9781501870842 (ebook) | ISBN 9781501870835 (hardback w/jacket)
Subjects: LCSH: Antisemitism. | Jews—History—1945- | Christianity and antisemitism.
Classification: LCC DS145 (ebook) | LCC DS145 .M64 2019 (print) | DDC 305.892/4—dc23
LC record available at https://urldefense.proofpoint.com/v2/url?u=https-3A__lccn.loc
.gov_2018022202&d=DwIFAg&c=_GnokDXYZpxapTjbCjzmOH7Lm2x2J46Ijwz6Yx
XCKeo&r=ox0wiE5wyqlD4NWBvXI_LEW57Ah1_xv-dTElReAYRyw&m=YfCMM89R
1eM4V97V22NMmSOzgJuCmKyq3XuiiL9w1RU&s=3JTCDcvlHpe1MEHQbzIST2Ap
DsUqeuzruDqzPcJgm7Q&e=

19 20 21 22 23 24 25 26—10 9 8 7 6 5 4 3 2 1
MANUFACTURED IN THE UNITED STATES OF AMERICA

Contents

Contents

Author's Note

I wrote the book you have in your hands in the summer and fall of 2017. The images of the rallies in Charlottesville were still fresh in our collective memory. The hate and the rhetoric, the torches and the anger seemed out of place in what at least our public world was like. It was one more very visible step in the increasing rise of anti-Semitism since the turn of the century.

Now as this book is going to print, we are living in the aftermath of the shooting at Tree of Life Synagogue in Squirrel Hill, Pennsylvania, where eleven Jewish worshippers lost their lives. I cannot know what will have happened in the domestic or international landscape by the time you are reading this, but I do know that the urgent call to build bridges and stand together against hate is clearer than ever.

Rabbi Evan Moffic

Other Abingdon Books by Rabbi Moffic

What Every Christian Needs to Know About Passover

*What Every Christian Needs to Know About
the Jewishness of Jesus*

Shalom for the Heart

Introduction

Last August, an acquaintance at a local church asked for a meeting. I knew her because her son had married someone Jewish, and they and their son had joined the synagogue where I serve as rabbi. When we sat down in my office, she held back tears and said, "I'm scared. I'm scared for my grandson. I want to know he will be okay."

I knew very little about her background, and I wasn't sure how to reply. So, I asked, "Why are you scared? What happened to your grandson? He seemed okay last time I saw him."

She answered, "He's Jewish."

Oh, I thought to myself. *She's scared because his parents are not raising him in the church. She wants to make sure he is getting a good religious education.* Her concern is not uncommon. I've met with many mothers and grandmothers in similar circumstances. She did not know much about Judaism, I surmised, and was concerned about her grandson's spiritual fate. Was he going to learn about the Bible? Was he going to feel close to God?

"It's okay," I replied. "His parents are wonderful people. You can be sure they are giving him a strong religious education. And remember: Jesus was Jewish, and I even wrote a book about it. I'm happy to give you one." I got up to get a copy of my book on the Jewishness of Jesus and brought it to her.

She looked at me strangely. She seemed to not understand anything I had just said. So, I continued, "I'm sorry. I don't mean be rude. I'm also happy to talk with your pastor about ways we can remind your grandson of his Christian heritage as well." She continued to look at me strangely.

"Am I missing something?" I asked.

She replied, "He's Jewish. That's fine. That's wonderful. I know he will get a good education at this synagogue and will be close to God. But just look around the world, Rabbi. So many people hate the Jews. Look at what happened in Charlottesville. Look at what's happening in Israel. Look at how many people have forgotten about the Holocaust. I am worried about his safety . . .

"Rabbi," she continued, "why is there so much anti-Semitism? Why are the Jewish people always hated and attacked? Why?" Tears rolled down her face.

That's where this book began. It is my answer to her question. It is a look at history's most enduring hatred. In this book, I explore how anti-Semitism affects Jews—but I also argue that anti-Semitism is not just a Jewish problem. It affects all of us. And it threatens not only physical safety and security.

Anti-Semitism is a litmus test of the social fabric—anti-Semitism's uptick usually goes hand in hand with other social and political problems, like political divisiveness, suppression of basic rights, and increased violence.

What Is Anti-Semitism?

As the grandmother of my congregant saw, anti-Semitism is growing today. Anti-Semitic incidents increased by 86 percent in the first quarter of 2017![1] Many of the rioters in Charlottesville, Virginia, in August 2017 carried signs that said, "Jews will not replace us." Anti-Semitism is a core value of both the alt-right movement and the Far Left, and anti-Semitism underpins many commonplace tropes that at first blush seem to be apolitical and unrelated to Judaism. But what, exactly, is anti-Semitism?

Anti-Semitism is hostility toward Jews. It appears in behavior, words, political policies, economic transactions, and religious practice. Anti-Semitism can even appear when Jews are not present, as was the case in Japan during the early twentieth century, when people expressed hostile views of Jews even though they had never met one. In addition, certain actions can be anti-Semitic in *effect* but not *intent*. For example, someone can say, "The Jews killed Jesus" without thinking he or she is saying something hostile toward Jews. But as we will see, this belief has had destructive and deadly consequences.

We also need to point out that *anti-Semitism* is not technically the right term for referring to persecution of Jews because Jews are not the only Semitic people. Others throughout the Middle East are considered Semites. But we will use *anti-Semitism* throughout the book because it has come to be widely understood as referring to hostility toward Jews.

While certainly a prejudice, anti-Semitism is not synonymous with bigotry or racism. Judaism is not a race, because a person can convert into Judaism, but Judaism is, in part, an ethnicity, because a person is automatically Jewish if his or her mother is Jewish. Thus, anti-Semitism is not simply a traditional form of racism or religious bigotry. It is both and more. Even more importantly, history suggests that when anti-Semitism grows, so does racism, bigotry, sexism, and the other kinds of divisions we see spreading around the world today. As anti-Semitism grows, so does the erosion of our faith, culture, and core values. A world not safe for Jews is a world not safe for anybody. Hence the title of this book. "First the Jews" is a quotation from the apostle Paul, who wrote in the letter to the Romans that God would save all who believed, "first the Jews" and then the Gentiles (1:16 GNT). But "first the Jews" is more than a biblical statement about God's saving power. It is also a reminder that Jews are the first targets of tyrants. An old Jewish proverb says that when a Jew coughs, the world catches a cold. Put differently, treatment of Jews is a barometer for the health of a society.

The Journey

We begin the book by looking at the present moment and answering the question, Why has anti-Semitism surged over the last two decades? In doing so, we look at recent events on the left and right of the political and social spectrum: The anti-Semitism articulated by the alt-right is a new phenomenon, but not a surprising one—reactionary groups thriving on public anger and division have often persecuted Jews. However, the Left's consistent targeting of Israel—which, as I argue in the next chapter, has anti-Semitic components—has led many Jews to feel betrayed by people they thought were peers and friends. It's one thing to experience anti-Semitism from neo-Nazis. It is another thing to see it among people you trust.

Then we must ask the broader question: Why does anti-Semitism exist at all? Why is it the world's longest-lasting and most persistent hatred? My answer is the "Big Five"—the five rationales used throughout history for anti-Semitism:

- Jews are different.
- Jews killed Jesus.
- Jews are greedy.
- Jews are an inferior race holding back scientific and human advancement.
- Jews are Western imperialists.

Next, I suggest how we can best respond to anti-Semitism today. I focus in particular on the dangers that a decline in religious practice and in political civility pose for creating the kind of culture in which religious differences can coexist. I argue that our future depends on moving away from identity politics—a political discourse in which we reductively identify groups as either wholly "privileged" or wholly "oppressed"—toward an appreciation of the other and a focus on common ground.

Interspersed throughout is my personal story as a rabbi—how experiencing and witnessing the rise of anti-Semitism changed me from naive to committed, from a leader focused on serving only his own community to a rabbi committed to teaching people of all faiths.

Ten years ago, I didn't teach much about anti-Semitism, but I increasingly feel it's urgent for Americans of all religions and no religion to address together the rise in anti-Semitism—and to consider what the consequences will be if we do not. Will we look back and see our era in the same way we look back and see the Europe of the 1930s? Or will we learn the lessons of the Holocaust and combat the resurgence of history's oldest hatred?

Surprise

The Rise of Left-Wing Anti-Semitism

In 1960, actor Paul Newman starred as Ari Ben Canaan in a movie called *Exodus*. Directed by Otto Preminger and based on a novel of the same name by Leon Uris, it tells about the young nation of Israel through the story of Ben Canaan's family. It took its name from the second book of the Bible—Exodus—but also from a ship of refugees during the Holocaust. In the film, this ship is preparing to leave for Palestine, which was then under British control. But the British prevent it from leaving the harbor. The ship's passengers throw their food overboard and go on a hunger strike until the British relent.

The symbolism is clear. These Jews are leaving the old world of slavery and oppression—the world of Europe that produced the Holocaust—and making their way to the promised land, Israel, to build a vibrant new country. They are willing to do anything to live in freedom. While not ignoring the complexities of forging a new Jewish state in a place already inhabited by communities of Arabs, the film highlights the Jewish people and the Jewish spirit—Jews' relentless and inspiring determination to rebuild an ancient faith almost destroyed by the Nazis.

I first saw *Exodus* in seventh grade at my synagogue Sunday school. It was a staple of synagogue religious schools in the 1980s and 1990s. We were learning about the Holocaust and the founding of the state of Israel. The film was moving, and I remember asking my grandparents to share the memories of Israel becoming a state. A few years later, my grandfather took me and two cousins on a trip to Israel designed for grandparents and grandchildren. I read the novel *Exodus* before leaving. On the plane, I met one of the grandfathers, who was also reading the book. He told me he read it on the plane every time he traveled to Israel, and this was his fifteenth trip.

For decades, the book and film deeply shaped the way many Americans, of all religions, thought of and felt about of Israel: Israel was a country of hope and redemption, and a moral beacon to the world.

But not anymore.

Last year I listened to a talk by Professor Shaul Magid. He teaches in the religious studies department at Indiana University. For two decades, he showed *Exodus* as part of his Introduction to American Jewish History class. About ten years ago, he said, students began to walk out of class during the film, saying they were offended that he was promoting Israeli propaganda. According to Magid, even those students who did not walk out said that they found little inspiration or insight in the film and that it did not reflect their views of Israel. Instead of heroically emerging out of the ashes of the Holocaust, they said, Israel oppressed Palestinians. Professor Magid ultimately stopped showing *Exodus* because it alienated students from the class.

The students' reactions are emblematic of the way Israel is seen by many on the political and social left in America, including among many Jews. Of course, there are exceptions. But as one sociologist who has done numerous studies of American Jews and Israel has said wryly, "Israel is a red state, and American Jews are a blue country."[1]

Beginning

Universities often serve as the vanguard of the Left, and it is there that Israel became a focus of ire beginning in the early 2000s. Protests against pro-Israel advocacy groups and support for calls to divest university assets from companies operating in Israel are common at most major universities.[2] The majority of these protests articulate the thoughtful, reasoned criticism one could comfortably see from left-wing political parties in Israel. A growing fringe, however, reflects and promotes a sometimes veiled and sometimes pointed anti-Semitism, applying many of the two-thousand-year-old anti-Jewish stereotypes to the state of Israel. This chapter helps us make sense of this leftist anti-Semitism.

The American political left initially supported the state

of Israel. Israel's founders embraced a socialist ethos, with nationalized health care and strict labor laws. Through the 1950s and early 1960s, Israel's collective farms, known as kibbutzim, attracted praise and emulation from progressive groups around the world. And as we noted in discussing *Exodus*, Israel itself was seen as a heroic effort of an oppressed people to survive after the Nazi onslaught.

But that sympathy diminished rapidly after the 1967 Six-Day War. In six days, Israel's army defeated several Arab countries and tripled the amount of land it controlled. Israel was no longer the beleaguered, tiny country struggling in the Middle East. It was a growing power with nuclear weapons. Over time—and especially once Israel elected its first conservative government in 1977—progressive support diminished.

This decline was not universal or all-encompassing, and many progressive Jews in America still maintained support for the existence of Israel and even for Israel's conservative governments. But as Israel shed some of its socialist economic policies and grew more powerful militarily, progressive concern intensified. By the first decade of the 2000s, the fissures between an Israel led by more right-wing parties (as of this writing, conservative prime minister Benjamin Netanyahu has led the country for thirteen years) and an American Jewish community tied to progressive allies had become more acute.

A Warning at Harvard

The first public figure to call attention to this leftist anti-Semitism in the US—especially to the forms of left-wing anti-Semitism that are based on American campuses—was then Harvard president Lawrence Summers. On September 21, 2002, as the school year began, Harvard students, and some professors, began to call for the board of overseers to divest parts of the university's substantial endowment from companies operating in Israel. Those professors and students cited Israel's "human rights violations" and oppression of Palestinians. In the wake of these protests, Summers said that "serious thoughtful people are advocating and taking actions that are anti-Semitic in their effect if not their intent. Where anti-Semitism and views profoundly anti-Israeli have traditionally been the primary preserve of poorly educated right-wing populists," he added, "profoundly anti-Israel views are increasingly finding support in progressive intellectual communities."[3]

As Summers pointed out, in America anti-Semitism has often been "the primary preserve of poorly educated right-wing populists."[4] Figures such as David Duke and Charles Lindbergh, and groups such as the John Birch Society and Ku Klux Klan, served as their most prominent leaders. In contrast, it was left-leaning politicians like Franklin Roosevelt and liberal Hollywood producers whose policies and films challenged anti-Semitic views. Liberal universities were also among the first major institutions to fight anti-Semitism by abandoning quotas on Jewish students after the Second World War. Anti-Semitism was a problem of the Right rather than the Left.

But Summers was seeing a different alignment. This new anti-Semitism of the Left described Israel in the same way earlier anti-Semites had described the Jewish people: all-powerful, sneaky, deceitful, and arrogant and greedy abusers of others. This leftist anti-Semitism strays beyond reasonable political criticism of a nation's government and makes outlandish charges—for example, that Israeli soldiers are poisoning children and targeting civilians in combat.

The new, leftist anti-Semitism presents a unique challenge: How do we distinguish legitimate criticism of Israel from anti-Semitism? In other words, when is it fair to call leftist critiques of Israel "anti-Semitic"?

To be sure, it is not always easy to decipher the difference between reasonable political criticism and anti-Semitism— there's no obvious, bright line. Sometimes harsh words about Israel are simply a means of expressing a legitimate political point of view. Later in this chapter, we will clarify the times when political criticism crosses over into anti-Semitism. But what is important to understand as we begin this discussion is that one sign of anti-Semitism is the depiction of all Jews as responsible for the actions of some Jews. When those on the left charge Jews living outside of Israel with responsibility for what they believe are the crimes of the Israeli government, we edge into the terrain of anti-Semitism.

Chicago Parade

Here's one recent example of this type of anti-Semitism in my own city: the targeting of Jewish symbols at a gay pride parade.

Like many big cities, Chicago hosts different gay pride

parades. One of the parades is known as the Dyke March. For twenty years, a small group of Jewish activists has participated in the march; in 2017, Jewish participants joined as usual. As the march began, however, one of its organizers asked three Jewish participants to leave. When these three marchers asked why, the organizer said the flag they were carrying—which featured a Jewish star—"made people feel unsafe" and stated that the march itself had a "pro-Palestinian" and "anti-Zionist" perspective. When they pointed out that they were marching as gay American Jews proud of being Jewish, not as Israelis, the organizers again asked them to leave.

Several of them did leave, and when one of them wrote about their experience in a newspaper, one of the organizers took to the march's public Twitter account and accused the Jews who had left the march of being "Zios"— an epithet for Jews popularized by Ku Klux Klan leader David Duke and commonplace in white-supremacist speech. "Zio tears replenish my electrolytes," read the Twitter post. So a gay-rights march targeted American Jews for being proud to be Jewish, and then, in the social media exchange after the event, used anti-Semitic terminology to revel in Jewish suffering.

Of course, the march organizers probably would not say they kicked out the Jewish activists for being proud to be Jewish. The organizers might say they thought that Jewish marchers automatically supported the government of Israel—and since the march's organizers described themselves as pro-Palestinian, the organizers might have concluded that the Jewish marchers and their flag symbolized a view inconsistent with the march. But the marchers were not Israeli, nor did they carry an Israeli flag. They were kicked out simply for displaying the fact that they were Jewish. That's anti-Semitism, not anti-Zionism.

For some people on the left, any Jew who identifies as a Zionist merits criticism, because the label "Zionist" is understood to indicate either ethnocentrism or support for and complicity with the current right-wing government of Israel, or both. Indeed, some on the left think that anyone identifying as a Zionist is perforce a racist (a view the United Nations held for decades until it formally rescinded the "Zionism is racism" resolution in 1991).5 But "Zionist" is a label I've claimed since I first saw *Exodus*, and to my mind, it simply means that I am committed to the existence of Israel as a state where Jews from around the world can live and govern themselves in freedom. I was shocked when I first realized that many leftists, including friends of mine, might think my attachment to the term *Zionist* is little better than proudly saying I'm a racist.

This came home to me while sharing the podium at an interfaith gathering with my friend Reverend Lillian Daniel, the author of *When Spiritual but Not Religious Isn't Enough*. In the middle of the discussion, she asked me if I was a Zionist. The question took me aback at first. *Of course I am*, I thought. *Do you believe in women's suffrage?*

Yet, as I looked around the room, I saw several people nodding their heads. They were wondering the same thing. To them, the word *Zionist* had pejorative connotations. It smacked of ethnocentrism. I explained that Judaism is not primarily a religion. It is a culture, a philosophy, and a people. It has a language and a land. If Zionism is feeling a personal connection to the nation of Israel, then being a Zionist is a core part of being Jewish—and for many, Zionism is also a part of being Christian! And, of course, Zionists can criticize the policies of the state of Israel. In Israel, many Zionists do so regularly and vociferously.

Because attachment to the land of Israel is a core Jewish value, when people on the American left suggest that Judaism is or should be a disembodied religion with no historic or present connection to a land and a state, it belittles both Jews and Judaism. Jews understand the land as an emblem of the intimacy between God and Israel; asking them to disavow or simply forget about that emblem would be akin to asking Catholics to give up the Eucharist.

Martin Luther King Jr. once said to a student who had made critical comments about Zionists, "When people criticize Zionists, they mean Jews. You're talking anti-Semitism."[6] So, anti-Semitism often masquerades as anti-Zionism. Again, one can criticize Israeli policy without partaking in either anti-Zionism or anti-Semitism. But to read all Jews as responsible for that Israeli policy is fundamentally anti-Semitic. It is like holding a man living in San Francisco responsible for the crimes of his first cousin in New York. Or, it is like calling someone a racist and then saying his siblings must be racists as well.

The Chicago Dyke March ejection is a perfect example of the anti-Semitic impulse to hold all Jews responsible for one group's anger with decisions made by the Israeli government. Another example occurred at Oberlin College. A group of liberal Jewish students wrote a letter to the school newspaper

9

after the president of the university spoke out against anti-Semitism on campus. These students accused the president of conflating anti-Zionism and anti-Semitism, and they suggested the fight against real anti-Semitism loses credibility when anti-Semitism is defined so broadly as to include protests against the state of Israel. Strictly speaking, they accused the president of watering down the meaning of anti-Semitism by describing criticisms of Israel as anti-Semitic. They insisted that liberal American Jews could be proudly pro-Palestinian.

But the responses to those students' actions proved their critics right. Shortly after their letter appeared, a group describing itself as "Students for Palestine" (SFP) disassociated themselves from any connection with these liberal Jews. They said SFP refrains from actions or letters on behalf of Jewish students because of Palestinian solidarity.

Think about this scenario for a second: Students for Palestine refrains from associating with Jewish students because of Palestinian solidarity. Being Jewish automatically makes one a supporter of (what the SFP sees as) Israeli oppression. No Jew can support Palestinian aspirations.[7]

This is a form of anti-Semitism because it demands that Jews choose between their Jewishness and their ideological sympathies. They can either be proudly Jewish or proudly progressive. Imagine if someone said no white person can ever support civil rights. Or that a male can either oppress women or renounce his gender. These are absurd choices. Yet left-wing anti-Semitism forces Jews to make a similar one.

This anti-Semitism we are seeing on US campuses and in marches like the Chicago Dyke March is new, but it partakes of a trope that has been a staple of anti-Semitism throughout history. In the late-eighteenth century, as the French Revolution began and its leaders proclaimed a new era of enlightenment and acceptance, French revolutionaries also said that Jews had to choose between identification with France and commitment to the Jewish people. One identity precluded the other. (We'll say more about this in chapter 8.) In the late-nineteenth and early-twentieth centuries, Socialist Jews in Russia faced a similar dilemma. Bolshevik leaders said religion had no place in a Socialist state, and Russian Jews sympathetic to Socialism could either give up their Judaism or remain part of the corrupt class. Many Jews fled Russia during this time, and others left Judaism. Even then, anti-Semitism persisted, as those Russian Socialists suspected of having a Jewish heritage had unique identity cards and were targeted by others. You could not be a socialist and be Jewish. You could not be a true French citizen and be Jewish. Today you can't be a real progressive and be Jewish. Or, at the very least, if you want to be progressive and Jewish, then you have to distance yourself from Israel and the ideals of the Jewish state.

This trend disturbs me not only because it resurrects old anti-Semitic views but also because it undermines American ideals and traditions. One of my heroes is Louis Brandeis. He was the first Jewish Supreme Court justice and a confidant of several American presidents. Brandeis was one of the great progressive leaders of his day and an ardent Zionist. He argued that America is a place where our different identities strengthen rather than undermine one another. Brandeis said his Jewishness helped him become a better American, and his

American ideals made him a better Jew. His success exemplifies America's embrace of religious diversity.

But now, those who claim to speak for America's highest values force Jews to make a choice between our faith and our politics. Brandeis would not recognize this kind of America. Neither do I.

Intersectionality

American progressives' hostility toward Israel—and the resulting marginalizing of Jews within various progressive communities—is part of a broader narrative. That narrative sees Jews as a privileged people oppressing others. To understand that narrative, it's helpful to think in terms of *intersectionality* a term coined in 1989 by Professor Kimberly Crenshaw. Crenshaw argued that her identity as an African American feminist could not be understood simply by studying the African American experience and women's experience. Rather, identities overlap. One form of social oppression changes the experience of another.

At its best, intersectionality helps us understand that we are made up of multiple identities. I am a Chicagoan, a Jew, a man, an American, a college graduate, and so on. None of these identities defines me in full. They overlap and interact, and it's healthy to acknowledge that they do.

At its worst, however, intersectionality leads, according to the *New York Times*, to a "caste system, in which people are judged according to how much their particular caste has suffered throughout history."[8] The more a particular identity

has suffered, the more its members have a right to speak out and demand change. Victimhood confers status.

At first glance, Jews would seem to benefit from this type of intersectionality. Jews have suffered oppression throughout history. And a 2017 study found that Jews are the number one victim of hate crimes in America. If having experienced oppression gives someone moral or political bona fides, Jews should be seen as politically and morally reliable, not as suspect.

But the perception among many progressives, as we have seen, is that Jews are complicit in the persecution of Palestinians. In addition, Jews are wealthy relative to other demographic groups. From an intersectional perspective, wealth lowers Jews' status because it preserves the oppressive structures in which we live. The wealthy, so the argument goes, manipulate and oppress others. This logic easily blends into an old anti-Semitic stereotype we will examine in chapter 7: Jews are money-hungry and oppress others to feed their greed. Thus, rather than lead us to a better understanding of Jewish history and identity, intersectionality has provided a new idiom for anti-Semitism—whatever their history, Jews today have money and are therefore current-day oppressors.

I doubt many who embrace intersectionality come to it with overt anti-Semitic views. But those who do can latch onto its language of blame and victimhood to frame Jews as the cause for economic and social ills and create alliances with others who do the same. Since intersectionality also holds that all social and political oppressions are linked, Jews get blamed for an amalgamation of social and economic problems. A

recent flyer at the main campus of the University of Illinois captured this tendency in one bold slogan: "Ending white privilege starts with ending Jewish privilege." The flyers included Stars of David with an arrow pointing to them and a caption, "the 1%."

Dangerous Praying

My wife, Ari, had a visceral experience of this mounting leftist anti-Semitism. She is a rabbi whose work focuses on Jewish and interfaith families who are not involved in synagogues. Her goal is to make Jewish ritual and Jewish practice more accessible to all people, whether or not they are part of a larger, organized community of faith. One Sabbath evening, she was invited to lead a prayer service at a conference in Chicago. Many of the organizations participating in the conference were progressive, including Israel's largest gay and lesbian rights group. She looked forward to the conference and worked enthusiastically on the service she was to lead.

On the day of the conference, Ari arrived for the prayer service and ascended the makeshift platform. She was leading the group in a song of praise when she heard loud shouts coming from the hallway. A riot had begun. Rioters were chanting loudly, "From the river to the sea, Palestine will be free," denying Israel's right to exist. They accused Israel of trying to cover up their oppression of Palestine by presenting themselves as gay-friendly. Israelis, they charged, were trying to hide Israel's evil ways by putting on a liberal-friendly face. And any Jews—even those enjoying a peaceful Sabbath

service—were part of the cover-up. Being Jewish and praying together with other Jews made one guilty of oppression.

Then it got worse. As one participant later recalled to a newspaper:

> They poured into the hallway from all different directions. We were huddled together to protect ourselves. There was a lot of pushing and shouting. They were very vocal about their hatred of Israel and what its stands for. It just kept getting bigger and bigger and, the more they couldn't get into the room the madder they became. I was shocked and mystified as to why they were protesting something when they didn't have all the facts. At the same time, I was not going to be intimidated by them.

When the group finally did get into the room, two of its leaders made their way to the podium and began calling conference attendees "oppressors and killers."[9]

My wife came home that night shaking and crying. I asked her what happened, and she told me the story. As I listened, I, too, grew shaken. I recognized the riot as an expression of an anti-Semitic trope—one more extreme and sinister than what I had seen in the media. For the rioters, not only was Israel an oppressive racist state but also that its supporters were canny and tricky, that while their ultimate motive remained oppression of the Palestinians, their aptitude for manipulation led them to present themselves as gay-friendly. Therefore, the conference organizers and attendees were, in the views of the rioters, two-faced manipulators.

That theme—Jews as two-faced, duplicitous, manipulative,

deceptive—has been a part of anti-Semitic literature since the early church's portrayal of Judas, the disciple who handed Jesus over to the high priests, who would ultimately have him killed. Judas presented one face to Jesus and the apostles— that of a loyal and trusted friend. But his true motives were to identify Jesus and get him into the hands of Rome. His final act—the kiss of death, where he identified Jesus to the Roman authorities by kissing him—captures that two-faced manipulation. A seeming act of love hid his true purpose.

The theme of Jews' duplicity reached new heights in the nineteenth century, with the publication of one of the modern era's most pernicious works of anti-Semitic literature—*The Protocols of the Elders of Zion*. The book was likely written in tsarist Russia in the 1860s. It quickly made its way into western Europe, and today it's also easily available in most Arab countries. *The Protocols* suggests a secret group of Jews meets annually in the Jewish cemetery in Prague in order to control the world through its banks and influence. Although they present themselves as concerned and patriotic citizens, they in fact seek only to enrich themselves. Jews act one way, but their motives belie their actions—they may seem patriotic, or loving, or friendly, but they are really a greedy and self-interested group of arrogant liars.

The protesters my wife faced that Sabbath may never have read or even heard of *The Protocols of the Elders of Zion*. And yet their fantasies of who Jews are resurrected *The Protocols'* themes: Jews are duplicitous, pretending to hold one set of values while sneakily working to advance an entirely different set of values.

Apartheid

We have seen the ways progressives shield anti-Semitism by calling it anti-Zionism. But what about those who say they are not anti-Zionist or anti-Semitic, but they believe Israel is committing massive human rights violations and becoming an apartheid state. Is that argument inherently anti-Semitic? Not always. But it can easily become so. And its language gives fuel to those who truly are anti-Semitic.

In a best-selling book in 2006, President Jimmy Carter made this exact argument—that Israel is becoming an apartheid state. "Apartheid" has a very precise meaning. It refers to a state in which races are legally separated by geography, employment, and marriage. Only certain groups can vote; people from one group are forbidden from marrying people from another group; certain areas are legally designated for specific populations.

Israel does not meet those requirements. As South Africa's chief rabbi, Warren Goldstein, points out, Israel

> accords full political, religious and other human rights to all its people, including its more than 1 million Arab citizens, many of whom hold positions of authority including that of cabinet minister, member of parliament and judge at every level, including that of the Supreme Court. All citizens vote on the same roll in regular, multiparty elections; there are Arab parties and Arab members of other parties in Israel's parliament. Arabs and Jews share all public facilities, including hospitals and malls, buses, cinemas and parks.[10]

That is not apartheid. So why does the charge arise?

Media Bias

The answer is a deeply ingrained and often unconscious anti-Semitism. That is what journalist Motti Friedman has argued in an analysis of media coverage of the Middle East. His analysis of contemporary journalism makes two important points: First, the contemporary media disproportionately covers Israel. Second, the underlying narrative of most news stories about Israel is slanted.

Friedman begins by telling the story in numbers and says that the number of staff assigned to a story indicates the importance of that story. For example, when he was with the Associated Press, "the agency had more than 40 staffers covering Israel and the Palestinian territories. That was significantly more news staff than the AP had in China, Russia, or India, or in all of the 50 countries of sub-Saharan Africa combined."[11] Yet, he continues, "in all of 2013, the Israeli-Palestinian conflict claimed 42 lives—that is, roughly the monthly homicide rate in the city of Chicago. . . . In contrast, in three years the Syrian conflict has claimed an estimated 190,000 lives, or about 70,000 more than the number of people who have ever died in the Arab-Israeli conflict since it began a century ago."

In other words, newspapers focus on what happens in Israel even though not much happens there compared to the rest of the world. Through disproportionate coverage, newspapers magnify events in Israel and focus the world's critical gaze there.

So why does that matter? Why is coverage of Israel more than simply a matter of editorial discretion? As Friedman points out, journalists always have an underlying narrative. Truly objective journalism is impossible because journalists tell stories, and stories rely on a narrative. Even articles that simply list facts about Israel would have an underlying narrative that helps the author determine which facts to include. Today, journalists can pick from several basic narratives about Israel. They could argue Israel is a tiny democracy of six million people fighting for its survival in an overwhelmingly autocratic Middle East of three hundred million. They could argue that Israel, whose neighbor is the Hamas-run government in the Gaza Strip, is on the front lines of the war against violent extremist Islam. But most Western reporters' default narrative is that Israel is a powerful aggressive force dominating the passive Palestinian population and foreclosing any possibility of peace through extremist political leaders, military oppression of Arab civilians, and continued expansion of settlements in Palestinian lands. This framing shapes the headlines and content of stories, and it portrays Israelis as the stronger party and the critical barrier to peace in the Middle East. The large staff reinforces how destructive Israel's behavior is for the world.

According to Friedman, this dominant narrative is a modern retelling of a morality play with a familiar villain: the Jews. As Friedman wrote, those in the West focus on racism, colonialism, and militarism as the biggest problems we face today. When society thinks it has moved past these problems into a "post-colonial, post-militaristic, post-ethnic dream-world," they must have a scapegoat when something bad happens. So, they focus on Israel, the world's only Jewish country, as a symbol of evil, even though Israel has done more good and less harm than any other country on the planet.[12] The concept of narrative is a critical one because we think and process information in stories, and every story needs a villain. In the story mainstream journalists tell of the Middle East, Israel is the villain. The Jewish state fits neatly into this role because Jews have been portrayed as the villain throughout history. Whether consciously or not, journalists are retelling an old story in a new era.

BDS

Perhaps the most destructive instance of this one-sidedness and implicit anti-Semitism is the Boycott, Divestment, Sanctions (BDS) movement prevalent on college campuses. Supporters of BDS want universities, states, and companies to divest their assets from and refuse to do business with companies operating in Israeli territories. Extreme supporters of BDS want such entities to refuse to do business with any company operating in Israel itself.

I first encountered the BDS movement when I got an email in mid-April 2015 from an old friend. He and I were the only Jewish members of our fraternity at Stanford, and we had stayed close over the years. "Have you heard," he wrote, "about the anti-Semitism happening on campus?"

Molly Horowitz, a young Jewish woman from Paraguay running for the Stanford student senate, had become subject to a barrage of hostility because of her religion and vocal support for Israel. Prior to the election, she had been asked by a coalition of student groups known as the Stanford Students of Color whether her Jewishness made her biased toward Israel. Shocked by the question, she soon told the *Stanford Daily* about her experience, adding that the Stanford Students of Color Coalition forbade candidates it endorsed to affiliate with any Jewish student organizations. Her story made it to the front page of the *New York Times*, and it highlighted the palpable hostility felt by active Jewish students on many college campuses.[13]

At that time, the student government had just voted to urge the university's board of trustees to divest from companies operating in what are deemed "occupied territories" in the West Bank of Israel. The motion received 66 percent of the vote of the student senate and was spearheaded by an organization called Students Confronting Apartheid by Israel. They claim Israel illegally occupies "Palestinian land" and engages in systematic discrimination. They also claim that Israel is a racist state because it privileges Jewish residents at the expense of others. They point to Israel's Law of Return as an example of the country's racist character. The Law of Return, passed at the state's founding in 1948, permits any Jew to immigrate and become a citizen of the state of Israel. It was passed three years after the Holocaust. Tens of thousands of Jews lived in displaced persons camps in Europe. They had survived the Second World War and the Holocaust. Their homes in Europe were now occupied by others. They could not return to live among people who had tried to slaughter them. Unless they had relatives in the United States or another allied country, they had no place to live—Israel was their only possible home.

The Law of Return has stood for seventy years, and it has not prevented non-Jews from becoming Israeli citizens. Hundreds of refugees from violence in Africa have come to Israel, as have refugees from Asia. Arabs also make up nearly 20 percent of the country's citizens. So, Israel has a particular immigration policy for Jews but also has a mechanism for the immigration of non-Jews. Even the Law of Return is more open than it might seem at first blush: after all, Judaism is a religion to which any person can convert and thereby become a citizen of Israel through the Law of Return.

As she reflected on the experience of anti-Semitism on campus, Molly Horowitz revealed that she felt forced to clear her Facebook page of any references to Israel. She felt she and other Jews would become targets of hate and discrimination. Indeed, two weeks after the story about Molly appeared in Stanford's newspaper, swastikas were painted on a fraternity house at the center of campus.

Such anti-Semitic expressions have not been limited to the Stanford campus. In 2015, when Northwestern University was considering divesting from Israel, students discovered swastikas spray-painted on the fifth floor of the library. Soon thereafter, racist comments were spray-painted on the library's fourth floor.

These are just two examples of a widespread phenomenon. Some, even in the Jewish community, dismiss BDS as an example of idealistic college students trying to make a point. To call BDS activism anti-Semitic, they say, is to make a mountain out of a molehill. But even a frequent critic of Israel, Thomas Friedman of the *New York Times*, said, "Criticizing Israel is not anti-Semitic, and saying so is vile. But singling out Israel for opprobrium and international sanction—out of all proportion to any other party in the Middle East—is anti-Semitic, and not saying so is dishonest."[14]

3D Discrimination

To be sure, distinguishing criticism from anti-Semitism is not always easy. We do not have a hard-and-fast rule for saying one statement is anti-Semitic but another is legitimate political criticism. The closest we have is what refugee activist and former Israeli foreign minister Natan Sharansky called the 3D test. The three Ds stand for *demonization, double standards,* and *delegitimization.*[15]

Demonization is scapegoating Jews for the world's problems and promoting conspiracy theories, such as "Jews control the media." When applied to Israel, demonization is the idea that Jews poison Palestinian schools or seek to hook Palestinian children on drugs, charges that have both been promoted in mainstream Arab publications. Demonization frequently takes the form of exaggerating Jewish power through rhetoric and imagery.

Double standards develop when a person or group criticizes Israel and only Israel without any reference to actions of other countries or communities. Boycotting Israel in the name of universal human rights without reference to ongoing persecution in Syria, Saudi Arabia, and Iran exemplifies this form of anti-Semitism.

Delegitimization is attacking the Jewish people's right to

23

self-determination. Those who say that the state of Israel is a threat to humanity or that it lacks any legal basis are engaging in this form of anti-Semitism. As we will see momentarily, a document from the Presbyterian Church questioning the UN resolution establishing Israel is an example of this form of anti-Semitism.

Again, distinguishing anti-Semitic rhetoric from legitimate criticism of Israeli policy is not always easy. But Sharansky's categories can help each of us read the news with greater clarity and understanding, and they can make our legitimate criticisms more lucid and compelling.

Mainline Churches

Over the last two decades, several of the nation's largest mainline Christian denominations have embraced varying degrees of BDS. The most prominent and comprehensive was the Presbyterian Church (USA), which passed a resolution in 2014 committing its $8 billion endowment to "selectively divest" from companies that it claims "further the Israeli occupation in Palestine." The denomination did not include a request from Jewish groups to recognize Israel as a Jewish state, and it advised congregants to read a document called "Zionism Unsettled," which recapitulated many core anti-Semitic themes, among them the idea that the Israeli "occupation" of Palestinian territories is the root of all the violence between Israelis and Palestinians.[16]

The following weekend, the pastor of my neighborhood's largest Presbyterian church came to the synagogue, where we had a dialogue. She reminded me that the vote was close (310–303) and that the denominational leadership did not speak for all of its three million members. But she also noted that many in the church share the feeling that Israel is the aggressive Goliath of the Middle East, threatening the small and beleaguered Palestinians. In this narrative, the Palestinians are a people violently pushed out of their homes, walled into small neighborhoods, and left to the mercy of their powerful oppressors.

I felt torn. I saw her point of view, and like many Jews, I empathized with the Palestinians' plight. At the same time, I know Palestinians have often been used as pawns by Arab states in their demonization of Israel. With funding for the families of suicide bombings and payments to Palestinian leadership, Arab governments encouraged the conflict as a way to deflect attention from their restriction of human rights. The more Israel can be depicted as the villain of the Middle East, the less attention their own regimes will receive. The problem was not the "occupation" of Palestinian lands; it was the lack of a desire for peace.

I went on to suggest that a Jewish person could understand the Presbyterians' resolution about divesting from Israel as an expression of anti-Semitism. Churches must be especially careful when talking about Israel because the state of Israel emerged out of Christian anti-Semitism. The Holocaust took place in overwhelmingly Christian Europe. As we will see in chapter 5, anti-Semitism was a prominent part of church teachings through the middle of the twentieth century. The reconciliation between Jews and Christians during the second half of the twentieth century is nothing short of miraculous, but it came on the heels of almost two thousand years of persecution. Therefore, when the church seems to reject the concept of a Jewish state, many Jews see it as a rejection of their identity, consistent with those centuries of persecution.

The Presbyterian Church seemed to do just that when it released its official study guide on Zionism, which questions the legitimacy of the 1947 United Nations resolution establishing the state of Israel. The guide does not question the establishment of any other state; just Israel. It singles out the Jewish state as uniquely illegitimate. It includes passages such as "Racism is the cornerstone of the Zionist project" and likens Israeli treatment of Palestinians to a "new crucifixion." This language is particularly noxious because, coming from a church, it echoes the idea that God has rejected the Jewish people—a notion that has led to horrific acts of violence throughout history.[17]

The Presbyterian Church has been joined by the United Church of Christ (UCC) in supporting divestment from Israel. Among the responses Presbyterian and UCC friends have offered me and other Jewish activists who have protested these resolutions is that some Jewish organizations supported them! And they are right. A few nominally Jewish groups, such as Jewish Voices for Peace, attended the Presbyterian Church conferences and wore shirts saying "Jews supporting BDS." Their presence raises an important question: Can a Jewish person be anti-Semitic?

Yes. Here's why: anti-Semitism is not just a rejection of Jews. It is hostility toward Judaism and Jewish values. It is a rejection of identification with the Jewish historical experience. Noam Chomsky, for example, has written for publishing houses whose books deny the Holocaust ever happened. He has consistently compared Israel with Hitler. Such statements remain anti-Semitic, even though they come from the pen of a Jewish writer.

We can understand the complexity of anti-Semitic Jews like Chomsky by examining a psychological phenomenon identified by French philosopher Jean-Paul Sartre in his book *Anti-Semite and Jew*. Sartre argued that the identity of "the Jew" is created by anti-Semitism. A Jew is someone whom the anti-Semite disdains. The only tie binding Jews is the hatred they receive from the larger society. Since the anti-Semite creates the Jew, how does Sartre define the anti-Semite? "The anti-Semite . . . is a man who [is] afraid. Not of the Jews to be sure, but of himself, of his own consciousness, of his liberty."[18] In other words, anti-Semitism is really a fear of oneself. Applying Sartre's thinking, we can say Jews who have imbued a sense of fear of or shame in themselves—fear or shame about being Jewish and about Jewish history—can become anti-Semites. Not all do, but when that fear is combined with a sense of alienation, as Chomsky has displayed in his writings, it is more likely. Fear of and alienation from one's identity can lead to hatred of it.

From Right to Left and Back Again

When I was growing up, right-wing Ku Klux Klan leader David Duke exemplified anti-Semitism in America. Duke remains a force in American politics, but when I think of anti-Semitism today, I do not think of right-wing neo-Nazis. When I think of anti-Semitism today, the first image that comes to mind is the left-wing rioters at my wife's Sabbath service. The first description that comes to my mind is progressive anti-Semitism.

Still, even as this strain of left-wing anti-Semitism has grown, its older cousin—the anti-Semitism of the Far Right—has renewed itself. That is the phenomenon to which we now turn.

Amy-Jill Levine

**Professor of New Testament and Jewish Studies,
Vanderbilt Divinity School**

Bastions of liberal politics interested in promoting "social justice," speaking "truth to power," and advocating for the "marginalized and outcast"—campus groups, academic professional societies, a few Protestant denominations, a few municipalities, some leaders in Britain's Labour Party—promote boycott/divest/sanction as the best approach to achieving peace in the Middle East, seek to delegitimize Israel as a colonial-settler state, and so deny Jews a place in the Jewish homeland. Some university professors refuse to write letters of recommendations for students who want to study in Israel; they thus place their politics ahead of the good of the student. One doubts that these same faculty members would refuse to write letters for students who want to study in countries that restrict women's rights, kill gay and lesbian people, put religious minorities into concentration camps, restrict immigration, or otherwise violate human rights.

This leftist discourse also conveniently denies the existence of Jews of color, whether in Israel or throughout the globe. When the state of Israel was founded, approximately 850,000 Jews were forced to flee from their homes in Morocco, Algeria, Tunisia, Egypt, Libya, Iraq, Yemen, Turkey, Lebanon, and Syria. Jews from the Middle East, North Africa, and Ethiopia account for slightly more than half of Israel's population, but their well-being is, again, irrelevant to the BDS scenario, whose promoters regard all Jews as white, elite, and Western. Zionism is, for many on the Left, indistinguishable from white supremacy and apartheid.

Jews who seek to enhance human rights find themselves unwelcome at the Left's table, whether Black Lives Matter or Chicago's Dyke March, or in university student governments; the only "good Jew" for such groups is the one who insists on Palestinian rights "from the river to the sea." In his 2018 *Contemporary Left Antisemitism* [Routledge], David Hirsh details the "antisemitism in social spaces which think of themselves as antiracist and democratic," the very places Jews have traditionally found a home.

Yet Jews who openly criticize Israeli policies such as settlement expansion, restrictions on non-Orthodox immigration, and women's ritual practices at the Kotel (Western Wall), become branded by many major Jewish organizations as anti-Israel or anti-Jewish. Rejected by the Left for their Zionist concerns even when they condemn Israeli policies, rejected by their own for their human rights interests even when they support a national Jewish homeland, liberal Jews find themselves increasingly ghettoized. In this scenario, the Left, the broader Jewish community, and liberal Jews all suffer.

2

Mainstreaming Hate

The Return of Right-Wing Anti-Semitism

O n Saturday, August 17, 2017, I received an email from Alan Zimmerman, the president of the largest synagogue in Charlottesville, Virginia. He described the scene outside of the synagogue on the previous Friday evening. "For half an hour, three men dressed in fatigues and armed with semi-automatic rifles stood across the street. Had they tried to enter, I don't know what I could have done to stop them. . . . Several times, parades of Nazis passed our building, shouting, 'There's the synagogue!' followed by chants of 'Sieg Heil' and other anti-Semitic language. Some carried flags with swastikas and other Nazi symbols."

He advised those in the building to leave via the back exit and also insisted that, in case the synagogue was attacked, they carry the Torah scrolls—the most sacred ritual objects

33

in Judaism—with them from the temple. At the same time, a few blocks away, several hundred others marched through the streets of the city. Some held signs saying, "Jews will not replace us." Some held tiki torches. Others held Confederate flags. Many identified as neo-Nazis.

The Charlottesville march was the largest gathering of white supremacists and neo-Nazis since the 1930s—but it was not an isolated incident. During the 2016 presidential election, journalists with Jewish-sounding last names were continually harassed on Twitter. A conference in Washington, DC, the weekend after the election ended with Nazi salutes. Hate crimes began to surge in 2015 and continued into 2016 and 2017. In the US, Jews top the victims of hate crimes by a wide margin.[1]

Addressing the rise in anti-Semitism has become the biggest challenge of my spiritual leadership. We have several Holocaust survivors and refugees from Nazi Germany in my congregation. After the Charlottesville march, one of them, who had just celebrated her ninety-sixth birthday, told me she felt more frightened than she'd ever felt since coming to the United States.

Another survivor, who had been a history professor, began teaching again so he could share the dangers he saw reappearing. He made two observations that made the hair on the back of my neck stand up. First, he noted that Hitler had blatantly attacked the legitimacy of the press and the courts. These attacks began right when Hitler entered office. In recent years, we have, of course, seen numerous examples of both congresspeople and the executive branch attacking the press and the judiciary. Second, the professor said the idea that "it can never happen here in America" is a fallacy. We sometimes become so comfortable that we forget what human beings are capable of doing to one another. To prove the point, he introduced me to an editorial that was published in a German Jewish newspaper on February 22, 1933:

> We do not subscribe to the view that Mr. Hitler and his friends, now finally in possession of the power they have so long desired, will implement the proposals circulating in [Nazi newspapers]; they will not suddenly deprive German Jews of their constitutional rights, nor enclose them in ghettos, nor subject them to the jealous and murderous impulses of the mob. They cannot do this because a number of crucial factors hold powers in check . . . and they clearly do not want to go down that road.[2]

How wrong that turned out to be! Liberal democratic institutions around the world are fragile. And these institutions do not sustain themselves. They can collapse without awareness, resolve, and action.

The Alt-Right

What explains the rise in anti-Semitism over the last two decades? We live in a time of rapid change, and history suggests that in times of instability, anti-Semitism rises. But several unique factors particular to our time and place underpin the surge in anti-Semitism: the damage caused by the great recession of 2008, the mounting gap between rich and poor around the world, the rise of radical Islam—and the emergence of the alt-right.

When I first heard this term, I shook my head in confusion. "Alt" is a key on a computer. What does it have to do with politics? In fact, the computer keyboard gives us a clue. On the keyboard, pressing the Alt key gives another key a different function. So, when it comes to the political right, the alt-right gives the old Right (which the alt-right sees as weak and too intellectual) a new function, a new task to perform, and new capacities. That new function is restoring the white identity of America.

First, some definitions. The alt-right is a growing group of white nationalists and white supremacists who attack both traditional conservative and progressive political views. They organize online, though they have connections with certain institutions and journals. In addition to arguing against racial integration and equality, their primary target is what they call "political correctness," and they relish in "triggering" people by using language and concepts long shunned by mainstream politicians.

Several prominent leaders and wings of the alt-right are also explicitly and virulently anti-Semitic. They believe that Jews represent global banks and institutions at odds with American national interests. According to the Anti-Defamation League (ADL), a Jewish organization founded in 1913 to fight bigotry, the alt-right uses the phrase "globalist elite" as a euphemism for "Jews." The alt-right also believes that Jews dominate the traditional mainstream media, which is a frequent target of its criticism. Indeed, in early 2016, many alt-right figures on social media began to put three parentheses, called echoes, around the names of prominent Jewish journalists and intellectuals—for example, (((Wolf Blitzer))). The point was to highlight how many Jews were part of the political and media establishment hostile to ordinary Americans. Their campaign drew so much attention that some prominent Jewish journalists on Twitter decided to put the parentheses around their own names. While they may have seen this as an act of protest, it served the alt-right's goal of highlighting the disproportionate Jewish representation in media. When combined with their demonization of the "MM" (mainstream media), this targeting gained traction. Some alt-righters even created a Google program that automatically put the three parentheses around *any* Jewish-sounding name (like Goldberg or Shapiro) on websites. It was downloaded thousands of times before Google blocked it.

Why does the alt-right target Jews? The first reason is tribalism. Alt-right leaders understand their purpose as defending an America threatened from within. To them, the Jew is the invidious outsider, primarily concerned with the interests of his own tribe. Jews look out for themselves. But Jews are uniquely dangerous because they assimilate effectively into native populations and then try to deceive them from within.

Jews also threaten the white Western society the alt-right envisions. "Europeans are Europeans and Jews are Jews and to call Europeans Jews is to insult them," says Richard Spencer, an alt-right leader who helped organize the Charlottesville riot.[3] Spencer envisions an American state comprising white people descended from Europeans, and he has stated that Jews have no place in that state. Even Jared Taylor, one of the alt-right's leading thinkers and writers, who is often seen as more sympathetic to Jews than other alt-right figures, sees an overrepresentation by Jews among individuals who have "tried to undermine white legitimacy."[4] In other words, Jews can never be true patriots because their ultimate loyalty is to their own tribe, which gives them the potential to destroy the white tribe from within.

The tribal basis of the alt-right's anti-Semitism differs from earlier American right-wing anti-Semitism because that earlier sentiment was primarily religious or social. American anti-Semites in the late-nineteenth and early- and mid-twentieth centuries saw Jews as outside of the American establishment—which was white, Anglo-Saxon, and Protestant—rather than outside of America itself. This is the kind of anti-Semitism seen in Oscar-winning films such as *Gentleman's Agreement*, where a Jewish man is excluded from certain neighborhoods and businesses because of his religion. It was the anti-Semitism of restricted country clubs and Ivy League quotas.

In the 1950s, some conservative groups, such as the John Birch Society, associated Jews with Communism and concocted conspiracy theories that named Jews as the enemies of America. Those conservative views, however, were rejected from the mainstream conservative movement as it evolved under the leadership of figures such as William F. Buckley. Buckley and other mainstream conservatives explicitly rejected anti-Semitism because they saw conservatism as a set of ideas, not an ethnic identity. They argued that America was not built on ethnicity but on ideas, and anyone committed to those ideas was welcome.

The alt-right, on the other hand, explicitly embraces white identity as part of its politics. And it rejects the earlier conservatives' focus on moral traditionalism and free-market economics. The alt-right even rejects the conservative movement's embrace of Christianity and the religious right. Understanding this rejection is critical to appreciating the influence and success of the alt-right and its leaders. It is also particularly surprising to many Jews, who traditionally associated anti-Semitism with Christianity. This is a topic we explore in great length in chapter 5, but we need a brief overview here to see how the alt-right departs from earlier expressions of anti-Semitism.

The Old Anti-Semitism

The religious right, which crystallized through Jerry Falwell's Moral Majority in the 1970s, remains a powerful force in American politics. While many of its members are pro-Israel and welcoming of Jews and Judaism, others are not. And sometimes the language of the religious right strikes Jews as anti-Semitic. Take, for example, the idea that "America is a Christian nation." That phrase strikes many Jews as anti-Semitic because it comes close to establishing an official religion from which Jews are excluded. So, while it may not be anti-Semitic in intent, it evokes that feeling in effect.

During the heyday of the religious right, some prominent evangelical leaders also called for Christians to actively try to convert Jews to Christianity. This is a complicated call for me, a Jewish leader involved in interfaith work, to assess. I understand that some Christians consider evangelism core to their identity, and for a Jew to ask them to set aside that core piece of identity strikes the Christian as the Jew wishing to eradicate something that's essential to Christianity. Nonetheless, as a Jew, I feel that being asked to convert to another religion is tantamount to calling for all of Judaism to be eradicated! For Christians who think that evangelism, including evangelism of Jews, is an essential part of Christianity (and not all Christians think this), this may be one of the indissolubly difficult parts of interfaith relations. Yet some aspects of evangelism to the Jews are not complex: it is not complicated to see that some of the language used by Christian leaders when calling for evangelism is deeply offensive.

In 1980, for example, the president of the Southern Baptist Convention, the largest Protestant denomination in the United States, said, "God Almighty does not hear the prayer of a Jew."[5] His comment echoed a doctrine subscribed to by most Christians throughout church history: supersessionism, the belief that God's covenant with the Jews was superseded by the new covenant sealed through Jesus. Because of their rejection of Jesus as Messiah, Jews were cut off from God, and now only followers of Jesus merited God's love. Supersessionism often becomes an implicit license for persecuting Jews because it frames Jews as lesser than Christians, cut off from God's love and care, and warranting punishment. As we will see in chapter 5, many of the most horrific anti-Semitic incidents stemmed from a supersessionist motivation. Calls to evangelize Jews are therefore problematic on two levels: they ultimately seek to eradicate Judaism, and they often cast Judaism as being wholly alien to the Christian God, even though that God is, of course, the God of Israel.

Jews have also expressed concern with some of the religious right's efforts to use the government to promote Christian identity and faith—these include calls for mandatory school prayer and funding for church-based soup kitchens and recidivism programs. To be clear, an aggressive commitment to right-wing politics and to using legislation and the courts to promote Christian values does not characterize the evangelical community as a whole, but it became a prominent part of the public perception of evangelicals with the rise of the Moral Majority in the 1980s. Jews saw in the religious right an attempt to undermine the separation of church and state in America, and that separation was important to Jews because they had experienced persecution at the hand of Christian states in Europe throughout history. Even though many Jews found some comfort in evangelicals' embrace of Israel, evangelicalism's emphasis on school prayer and vouchers that could use taxpayer money for religious schools alarmed many Jews who were worried their kids would feel alienated and "othered"—either pressured to convert to Christianity, or simply left with a lingering feeling that they didn't fit in with the American mainstream.

The Alt-Right Is Different

We can safely say, therefore, that the right wing of American political and cultural life has never been characterized by a straightforward and unambiguous acceptance and embrace of Jews and Judaism—but today's alt-right presents a different view of Jews and Judaism. The old model of religiously conservative Christian anti-Semitism has little to do with the alt-right's tribal aversion to Jews. Their hatred has a secular rather than religious foundation. As George Hawley put it in his masterful book on the alt-right,

> The Alt-Right is (for the most part) secular in its orientation and hostile to the politicized Christianity that dominated Republican politics since the late 1970s. For a generation, the secular left viewed the religious right as the greatest obstacle to the creation of an open and tolerant society; it now appears that the postreligious may be more threatening to fundamental liberal values than the religious right ever was.[6]

Part of the reason Hawley argues that the post-religious alt-right threatens fundamental liberties more than the religious right is that one of the parts of Christianity despised by the alt-right is Christianity's Jewish underpinnings! To the alt-right, Christianity is inherently tainted by its Jewish foundation. Jesus was Jewish, and so were the early disciples, and the fact that Jews play such an important role in Christian history and theology (even as Christianity has a long history of anti-Semitism) means that Christianity is weak and inconsistent with the strength and tribalism of the white nationalist ideal.

The alt-right's anti-Semitism resembles the perspective of Hitler more than, say, the view of Jews held by a Christian theologian such as Martin Luther. Luther (about whom I'll have more to say in chapter 5) rejected Jews because they did not convert to Christianity. His anti-Semitism, while extreme in its language, was consistent with earlier forms of Christian anti-Jewish beliefs. Hitler articulated his anti-Semitism in a different key. It was more tribal than religious, existential rather than theological. He despised Jews because he believed they tainted European civilization and blocked the rise of the German people. They were an inferior race threatening the survival of the superior race.

Like Hitler, the alt-right—especially leaders such as Richard Spencer—are attracted to the writings of Frederick Nietzsche, who said Christianity promotes an unhealthy morality that undermines the creation of the Über-mensch, the strong man, who can dominate his tribe and conquer others. Nietzsche also attacked Christianity's universalism—its openness to people of any race or ethnicity who accept its precepts. While Nietzsche was not an overt anti-Semite, his writings influenced Hitler and other Nazis who saw Judaism as the foundation of this dangerous Christian morality and believed only the elimination of the Jews and rejection of religion as a whole could restore the tribalism of the original Europeans. The neo-Nazi element of the alt-right embraces this perspective explicitly.[7]

Consider the phrase "Jews will not replace us," which was featured on the signs of many of the rioters in Charlottesville.

I lead a Facebook group called Christians and Jews Fighting Anti-Semitism, and several members of the group were confused when they saw those signs. They asked me what the signs meant. I had not heard the phrase before, but I had a feeling it represented more than economic jealousy, more than a feeling that Jews were replacing non-Jewish workers. It seemed something deeper was behind the phrase. I turned to a local scholar named David Nirenberg, who is a professor at the University of Chicago.

Nirenberg wrote a monumental tome titled *Anti-Judaism in the Western Tradition*. Surveying two thousand years of Western civilization, he suggests that although Western society has evolved over the centuries, it has always viewed Judaism as, in some form or fashion, a force to be defeated, marginalized, or eradicated. From early Christianity, which sought to replace the old covenant with the new, to the secular philosophes of the eighteenth century, who sought to replace religious dogma with scientific precision, the shapers of Western culture thought that Jews and Judaism had to be overcome—and in some cases destroyed—for Western culture to flourish.[8]

The Charlottesville rioters, Nirenberg suggests, saw Jews not only as a target in themselves but also as the enablers of the rise and prominence of African Americans, Latinos, and immigrants. Jews empower other groups that seek to undermine and supplant true white American culture. Their rich leaders, such as George Soros, are pulling the strings and using their influence and money to attack the social forces that keep immigrants and people of color in their place.

Alt-right websites frequently point to prominent Jewish political leaders and donors and entertainment figures to prove their point. Entire websites are dedicated to exploring the Jewish background and influence of prominent Jews such as Steven Spielberg, Ben Bernanke, and Gloria Steinem. As Jonathan Greenblatt, head of the Anti-Defamation League, says, "The extreme right considers many people their threat. But it always, always, always comes back to the Jews."[9] For the Charlottesville rioters, Jews must not be allowed to replace the white nationalist culture of America.

The alt-right's anti-Semitism targets both the right and left ends of the political spectrum. In 2015 and 2016, its biggest targets were Democratic socialist Bernie Sanders and right-wing radio host Ben Shapiro. These two agree on very little politically. Yet, both became the subject of memes using Nazi symbols on Twitter and Facebook. Both were depicted in Nazi death-camp gas chambers. The Anti-Defamation League reported that between August 2015 and July 2016, eight hundred journalists were the target of almost twenty thousand anti-Semitic Tweets. They concluded that many of the Tweets originated from accounts that also expressed support for Donald Trump. That doesn't mean the Trump campaign promoted anti-Semitism. Nor does it mean President Trump has anti-Semitic feelings or policies. But it does suggest that a few of his supporters engaged openly and proudly in anti-Semitic acts during the campaign. According to the *Washington Post*, the targeting of Jewish journalists on Twitter was the media story of the 2016 election.[10]

Elitism

One of the reasons journalists in general and Jewish journalists in particular are the targets of right-wing anti-Semitism is the alt-right's belief that institutions such as the *New York Times* and other "elite" periodicals have betrayed ordinary Americans by encouraging open borders, which help only the wealthy and connected. In the alt-right's view, Jews have been front and center in this effort. As Professor Hawley puts it, "The core concept of the [alt-right], upon which all else is based, is that Whites are undergoing an extermination, via mass immigration into White countries which was enabled by a corrosive liberal ideology of White self-hatred, and that the Jewish elites are at the center of this agenda."[11]

Defining who is part of the "elite" is not straightforward. Membership in the "elite" is often a matter of style rather than wealth or profession. For the alt-right, however, elite institutions include global banks, Wall Street, media companies, and quasi-governmental organizations, including the United Nations, the European Union, the World Bank, and NGOs (nongovernmental organizations, such as Amnesty International). The common thread is that these institutions transcend national borders.

In focusing on such institutions, the alt-right is drawing on a deep reservoir of American suspicion of international groups. The founding of the United Nations sparked outrage and conspiracy thinking among far-right groups such as the John Birch Society in the 1950s. They saw the UN as a Communist plot to undermine American sovereignty.

Enmeshed in this right-wing suspicion of international

groups is deep-seated anti-Semitism. This anti-Semitism finds expression in two particular arguments. The first is the belief in an international cabal of Jews who manipulate media and financial markets to enrich themselves. This cabal has no national loyalties and uses its wealth and clout to benefit Israel—Jews even concocted the Holocaust to generate global sympathy. In doing so, they have succeeding in intimidating their opponents and stifling all debate.

These arguments appear in popular books and journals of the far right; to an extent, they even seep into Hollywood. In the comedy *The Campaign*, starring Will Ferrell, the Republican candidate challenging Ferrell is told by a legendary political operator that when giving speeches, "never say anything bad about the Jews."[12] The joke works because it mocks the idea that Jews are so powerful that they are off-limits for any real criticism.

This joke leads us to the second anti-Semitic conspiratorial belief on the right—that wealthy American Jews control foreign policy through donations to politicians. Patrick J. Buchanan has made this argument, calling the American Congress "Israeli-occupied" territory,[13] as have many critics of the neoconservative wing of the Republican Party. Neoconservatives believe in an active American foreign policy, while conservatives in the Buchanan mold are more isolationist. They think America has shown too much support for Israel. Some of these conservatives attach the long-standing association of Jews with money (which we will explore in chapter 7) to long-standing fears that the country's elites are architecting a new global order that will hurt real Americans.

FIRST THE JEWS

One of the most extreme examples of anti-Semitic concerns about Jews controlling American foreign policy has been the suspicion, articulated by some alt-right groups, that the terrorist attacks of September 11, 2001, were organized by Israel, and that they were a pretense to get America involved in wars in the Middle East. Indeed, almost immediately after the events on September 11, articles appeared on prominent conspiracy sites and in Arab newspapers blaming Israel and its spy agency, the Mossad, for planning the attacks. They claimed Israelis who worked in the World Trade Center were told to stay home that day.

I was in Israel on September 11, and I saw these conspiracy charges covered in Israeli newspapers. They became so frequent that the Snopes website had to officially deem them false.[14] (Snopes is a website drawing from millions of users and sources to determine whether certain internet rumors, chain letters, and other controversial and conspiratorial arguments are true or false.) The logic, if it can be deemed logic, for blaming Israel for September 11 goes something like this: At a general level, wars in the Middle East serve the interests of elites, because elites prosper from the arms trade and from the massive spending that wars involve; ordinary Americans suffer because they are the ones who have to bear the human and financial costs of the wars. More specifically, Jews want to get the United States involved in wars in the Middle East to distract attention from Israel's treatment of the Palestinians. Israel also profits from such wars because they get more aid from the United States. American Jews, according to this account, are good at getting the United

48

States to do Israel's bidding. Their vehicle is the Israel lobby, which, in this account, has used fear and lies to manipulate US policy for decades, and their power has made representatives and senators pawns willing to do their bidding.

Again, we see variations of this argument from the Left and the Right. For example, John Mearsheimer, a liberal professor at the University of Chicago, cowrote a 2007 book titled *The Israel Lobby*, in which he argued that a small group of American Jews manipulates the political levers of power to support an aggressive and immoral Jewish state. The book contends the Israel lobby was largely responsible for America's invasion of Iraq because they believed it was in Israel's best interests.[15] Progressive groups in the United States and Europe supported Mearsheimer, even as several journalists compared his book to *The Protocols of the Elders of Zion*, the aforementioned nineteenth-century anti-Semitic book beloved of Hitler.[16]

As we see, anti-Semites on the left and the right agree that the Israel lobby is the vehicle through which American Jews get the United States to do its bidding; however, they differ on what they identify as its underlying motivation. Mearsheimer believes the Israel lobby is motivated by the interests of the extreme right in Israel. Ultimately, the lobby hurts American and Israeli interests because it leads America to subsidize extremists, preventing the emergence of a viable peace process.

Writers on the right, such as Richard Spencer, argue that the Israel lobby is simply a vehicle for Jewish power. It exists to enrich and serve whatever a small group of leading Jews deems is in the Jewish interest. Spencer also uses the creation of the Jewish state as an argument for white nationalism. He calls the alt-right a "white Zionist movement," saying that if Jews can set up an ethnic state and garner world support, then Caucasians have the same right. Spencer says he looks to Zionism as an example for the alt-right movement.[17]

This argument has shocked and frustrated some contemporary rabbis. A friend of mine who is a campus rabbi at Texas A&M University unwittingly encountered this argument directly from Spencer. Spencer was speaking at the university, and my friend—Rabbi Matt Rosenberg—asked him why he continues to teach such hate. Spencer responded by suggesting that Jews survive because they resist assimilation. They maintain their identity and culture. That's what he wants for whites. He does not promote hate. He promotes survival.

As he put it, "Jews exist precisely because you did not assimilate. . . . That is why Jews are a coherent people with a history and a culture and a future. It's because you had a sense of yourselves. I respect that about you. I want my people to have that same sense of themselves."[18] In other words, whites can learn from Jews how to preserve their identity in the face of pressure to give it up.

On the surface, the parallel between Jewish investment in self-preservation and Spencer's investment in white self-preservation might sound plausible. The problem is that Judaism is a religion and philosophy, not a skin color. And Israel is a state for all people—its declaration of establishment promises to "ensure complete equality of social and political rights to all its inhabitants irrespective of religion, race or sex."[19]

Spencer glossed over those parts of Jewish identity and maximized the ethnic parts of it—and he perhaps unwittingly provided fodder for far-left anti-Semitism by linking Israel with the alt-right.

More Elitism

Figures on the alt-right do not believe that Jews control only American foreign policy. They also see Jewish puppet masters on Wall Street and in Hollywood. Wall Street and Hollywood symbolize the coastal elites of America. The alt-right argues that this elite has maliciously pursued its own interests to the detriment of ordinary, hardworking Americans. Jews' disproportionate presence in both spheres is frequently highlighted in alt-right publications and propaganda.

Hollywood and Wall Street each represent a particular anti-Semitic trope for the alt-right. Hollywood represents Jewish immorality and sexual perversion. According to alt-right leaders such as David Duke and Andrew Anglin of the Daily Stormer website, Jews have used their control of film and television to infect the American people with their deranged perspective. They encourage premarital sex, homosexuality, and even sexual abuse.

In 2017, one of Hollywood's most prominent producers, Harvey Weinstein, was accused of numerous cases of sexual assault and harassment. The alt-right portrayed him as a symbol of Jewish control of Hollywood and pollution of American culture. Some alt-right figures even quoted the Jewish newspapers that portrayed Harvey Weinstein as reflecting some of the cultural stereotypes of American Jews. One newsmagazine—*Tablet*—said Harvey Weinstein was like a character out of a Philip Roth novel, a sex-obsessed Jewish male anxious about his power and taking out his anxiety by abusing young women.[20] The alt-right picked up on this portrayal, and as other prominent Jews in Hollywood and the media were accused of sexual harassment, the alt-right dialed up its conspiracy language. Andrew Anglin of the Daily Stormer—a long-standing anti-Semitic website newly energized by the alt-right and frequently appearing near the top of Google searches that include the word *Jew*—wrote "The Jews have made our nation into the global center of filth that they made Germany into in the 20s. And I just want you to remember this: back then, a bunch of guys got really . . . pissed off about it. And I am just going to tell you this: that didn't end well for the Jews. It isn't going to end well for them this time either."[21]

The alt-right's focus on Hollywood has the potential to gain greater traction because many mainstream conservatives believe Hollywood has promoted immoral ideas that weaken American families and faith communities. Hollywood is also a center for fund-raising for the Democratic Party, and Jews do make up a significant percentage of Hollywood writers, producers, and directors. That has been the case for almost a hundred years, because when the movie industry was founded, Jews were not able to enter many mainstream professions, such as law, business, and medicine. Hollywood was wide-open, and many children of Jewish immigrants—people like the Warner brothers—started their first studios. Jews such as Steven Spielberg, Ari Emanuel, and Larry David remain among its most visible directors, agents, and actors. As Hollywood becomes a target for anger, many Jews are caught in the crosshairs.

Along with other rabbis, I have been concerned about this trend. While Jews may be prominent in certain industries, we are a tiny percentage of the world population—about 0.2 percent.[22] To put that in perspective, as one scholar notes, the entire world Jewish population would be considered a small statistical error in the Chinese census.[23] Therefore, when a Jewish person receives significant negative media attention— as has happened with Harvey Weinstein and others—it almost feels as if a member of our family has been publicly shamed. We feel upset and angry. And we also feel concerned about further public backlash. We worry the public furor will taint the Jewish community as a whole.

The best response so far has been to state plainly and simply that sexual abuse and Hollywood have nothing to do with Jews and Judaism. Indeed, the teachings of our tradition stand in profound opposition to sexual abuse. Gal Gadot, the Israeli actress and star of *Wonder Woman*, made this argument and refused to attend a major Hollywood function honoring a Jewish director—Brett Ratner—accused of sexual misconduct. Jews are not monolithic in behavior or points of view. To say that Jews are—as the alt-right has and will likely continue to do—is anti-Semitic.

Wall Street

Hollywood is not the only place where stereotypes of Jews predominate. Since the 1930s, words and phrases such as *money power*, *alien*, *cosmopolitan*, and *Wall Street bankers* have been used as coded references to Jews. Indeed, the association between Jews and financial greed goes back thousands of years.

During the Middle Ages, as we will see in chapter 7, money lending was one of the few professions open to Jews and forbidden to Christians. Consequently, Jews became financiers of shipping (the primary means of trade) and frequently loaned money to local churches. When towns suffered economic decline, Jews were usually blamed. Writings from the time—such as Chaucer's *Canterbury Tales*—depict Jews as greedy and miserly. Shakespeare helped seal this image in *The Merchant of Venice* with the character of Shylock, who became an enduring symbol of the greedy Jew who would demand his pound of Christian flesh.

The economic downturn of 2008 and 2009 led to a resurgence of this symbolic connection between Jews and greed. A 2009 survey found that a quarter of all Americans believed Jews were at least moderately responsible for the financial downturn.[24] In 2010, Rush Limbaugh discussed Jews who voted for Obama. He argued Jewish liberals should rethink their support for Obama, who won about 75 percent of the Jewish vote in the 2008 election. Limbaugh's remarks traded on the stereotype of greedy Jewish Wall Street bankers: "There are a lot of people," he said, "when you say banker, people think Jewish. . . . To some people, bankers—code word for Jewish—and guess who Obama's assaulting? He's assaulting bankers. He's assaulting money people. And a lot of those people on Wall Street are Jewish. So I wonder if there's starting to be some buyer's remorse there."[25]

On a surface reading, these remarks might seem innocuous. Limbaugh thinks Jews should stop supporting Obama because they are the Wall Street bankers Obama is attacking. The problem is that Limbaugh perpetuates a harmful stereotype when he notes that "a lot of those people on Wall Street are Jewish." There are probably, as a percentage of the total, more Americans of Irish descent and Christians working on Wall Street than there are Jews. By singling out Jews, Limbaugh is playing on the old anti-Semitic stereotype of Jews controlling Wall Street and money.

The alt-right has gone even further. They have taken the Wall Street stereotype and emphasized its connection with immigration and globalization. This is not hard to do. Wall Street banks are global institutions. They foster trade and movement of money across borders. Flow of money and flow of people can reinforce one another, and the largest financial institutions have offices throughout the world. For the alt-right, therefore, they embody the lack of national loyalties and indifference to ordinary Americans. They have little respect for our borders.

According to those on the alt-right, global elites permeate both major political parties, the media, and Hollywood. But Wall Street takes the cake. Its leaders are perched at the apex of global power. Their greed motivates them to continue to undermine American sovereignty and funnel more of our wealth to their elite friends around the world. The alt-right's nativism and anti-Semitism come together in its perception of the global financial elite, and the alt-right continually glosses that financial elite as Jewish. Jews, therefore, represent the global banks enriching its leaders and ignoring national borders.

This isolationist anti-Semitism has a long history in America. Up until the present, the most anti-Semitic era in American history was the 1930s. The horror of World War I and the pain of the Depression soured many Americans toward involvement in foreign countries. They believed foreign nations had taken advantage of American generosity in Europe during the war and in our open borders prior to 1924, a year that saw the first major immigration restrictions. Jews, on the other hand, did not share this isolationist sentiment. They saw what was happening in Nazi Germany and felt American involvement was necessary. They struggled as immigration restrictions cut families off from one another. They supported President Roosevelt, and his election in 1932 generated more isolationist backlash.

My grandfather recounted sneaking into anti-Roosevelt rallies in the 1930s. He was a student at Marquette University in Milwaukee, and the crowd brimmed, he said, "with hate." They did not want the United States to enter into the war in Europe. They wanted to focus on putting food on the table amid the Depression and avoid repeating the disastrous experience of World War I, which left seventeen million dead and another twenty million people injured. He told me many of Milwaukee's most prominent citizens were at this rally, including some of his professors and the mayor.

My grandfather saw locally what was true nationally. Isolationism permeated the corridors of American power. In 1940, aviator Charles Lindbergh joined with Walt Disney,

Frank Lloyd Wright, and other prominent Americans to form a group called America First, which advocated neutrality in the war in Europe. Lindbergh accused Jews of pushing President Roosevelt toward war. Support for isolationism and suspicion of Jewish power and influence rose together. By 1938, 60 percent of Americans said in a poll conducted by the American Jewish Committee that they believed "persecution of Jews in Europe had been their own fault."[26] In a series of fourteen different polls between 1938 and 1946, one-third to one-half of respondents said Jews had too much power in America. America's entry in the Second World War in 1941 did not significantly reduce these percentages.

Over time, however, a recognition of the magnitude of the Holocaust, coupled with increased openness in American culture (openness that stemmed, for example, from reforms in immigration law that increased the diversity of American communities), eroded anti-Semitic practices, such as maintaining quotas for Jews at Ivy League universities and rebuffing Jews who served or sought to serve on major cultural boards. By the late 1960s, the perentage of Americans who held anti-Semitic attitudes hovered between 20 to 30 percent, and by 1998, that reached the low level of 12 percent.[27] The numbers began to climb in the 2000s, and they have continued to climb with the rapid growth of the alt-right.

What Next?

I am writing this book in 2018 as the election of 2016 fades into the past. Some of the heated rhetoric of the alt-right has diminished. One of the figures most associated with it—Trump campaign CEO and senior advisor Steve Bannon—has been fired and rejected by the president. One of the alt-right's most popular and charismatic spokesmen, Milo Yiannopolis, has been sidelined because of charges of pedophilia. Yet, a recent report says the majority of murders committed by extremists in America in 2017 came from white supremacists.[28] Such hate crimes continue to grow. Like a virus, anti-Semitism has a way of mutating and adapting.

Jake Owensby

Author of *A Resurrection-Shaped Life: Dying and Rising on Planet Earth* and Bishop, Episcopal Diocese of Western Louisiana

How should we respond to those who seek to annihilate us? That's the disturbing question posed by the rhetoric and violence of the alt-right to Jews, Christians, people of color, and anyone else whose being or ethos or creed opposes the supremacy of whiteness. (The absurdity of the very idea of "whiteness" calls for another essay at another time.)

Alt-right leaders disingenuously claim that their intention is to save white culture from annihilation by the pressures of multiculturalism. They justify their malevolence toward Jews, Christians, and brown-skinned people by portraying these groups as threats to the very survival of the white race. That theme was summarized by signs at Charlottesville that read "Jews will not replace us."

The alt-right strategy is insidious. They claim to be a marginalized, oppressed group demanding only what every other constituency deserves and demands: a right to exist and to have an equal voice in public discourse. To put this a different way, the alt-right wants a place at the table equal to everyone else.

There's just one problem. And it's a big one.

The alt-right actually seeks a place at the table in order to assert that no one else at the table is their equal. Eventually, their goal is to establish an all-white table and to exclude all others from it. They cynically use the principles held sacred by those of us working toward an inclusive society to dismantle that society from within.

In other words, the alt-right seeks to annihilate us.

In the interest of full disclosure, you should know that my mother survived the Nazi concentration camp Mauthausen. I am not an entirely objective observer. However, my mother's story brings crucial perspective to understanding the alt-right.

My mother was not a Jew. Neither was she Roma or homosexual or a member of a banned political party or any other minority targeted by the Nazis. She was Roman Catholic and fifteen at the time of her internment in the camp. Classifying her as socially undesirable, the Nazis sentenced her to death by work, starvation, and exhaustion. As Rabbi Moffic's title implies, when they come for the Jews, that's just the beginning. They're eventually coming for everyone not like them.

The Nazis represent perhaps the clearest example of the distorted, destructive white supremacist spiritual DNA. The alt-right embodies those ideological genes. And that genetic material trends always toward annihilation of the other.

So I return to the question. How do we respond to those who seek to annihilate us? We can remember what the philosopher Karl Popper called the paradox of tolerance. In short, tolerating intolerance will lead to the annihilation of tolerance. Bullies will be given free reign to silence those with whom they disagree.

In debates and civil demonstrations involving the alt-right, we should never suggest that there are fine people on both sides. To guard the dignity of every human being, we must reject out of hand any claims to the supremacy of one group over another.

3

An Optimist
Faces Reality

My Story

Do you ever think back and picture the good old days? Perhaps a church pew where you sat as a child or a chair where your grandfather relaxed? The place from childhood that, when you picture it, gives you a warm feeling inside?

For me, one of those places is the Jewish Community Center building in Houston, Texas. It is a sprawling complex with tennis courts, a gym, classrooms, racquetball courts, playgrounds, and a game room. The building was across the bayou from the home where I grew up. After school, I would head over with a few friends, play basketball or baseball, and hang out in the game room. I went to camp there all summer. It was a home away from home.

When I was eleven, we moved to Milwaukee, Wisconsin, to be closer to my grandparents. The JCC in Houston remained a cherished memory. Whenever I met someone from Houston, we would talk about the JCC, and the good vibes would return.

Then in 2017, I received an invitation to speak at a books and culture festival in Houston. The talk would take place at the JCC. I was so excited to visit and kept telling my wife and kids how amazing it was. Of course, I realized the hues had become more golden over time. I knew I was probably imagining the JCC as more glorious than it was. But the excitement remained.

A car picked me up from the airport and took me right to the JCC. The car drove past the bayou and turned onto the JCC's street. Then we were greeted by a huge cast iron fence. It surrounded the entire building. You could barely see the front doors and the fields in back. It reminded me more of an army base than a community center.

I was shocked. Then a bit angry. It felt as though my childhood home had been turned into a fortress. But I realized I was angrier at something deeper. Times had changed, and the iron fence represented that change. The Jewish community was more vulnerable. Earlier that year, a dozen JCCs had to be evacuated because of bomb threats. The relaxed security of the 1980s and 1990s, when we could run into the JCC through any of the dozen open doors, was over.

The surge in anti-Semitism has not just unsettled my childhood memories but has presented the greatest challenge of my spiritual leadership. How do I guide my people in responding to a threat many have not really experienced until now? How I do respond to a phenomenon that is so old yet feels uncomfortably new?

This unsettling (and unsettled) feeling started to take concrete form in 2010, when the FBI warned all Chicago synagogues about packages with explosives discovered on a cargo plane bound for the United States. Somehow they had also learned that two of these suspicious packages were bound for "Jewish places of worship" in Chicago. It turned out one of them was sent to the synagogue led by one of my closest rabbinic mentors.

The packages were eventually intercepted, but a pall of fear fell over the Chicago Jewish community. We all increased our security; we all felt a new fear. We looked more closely at the packages of toner cartridges arriving at the synagogue. We looked a little more suspiciously at unfamiliar faces in the building.

How do we respond to this new climate of fear? Do we turn inward, focusing primarily on our own security and interests? Do we circle the wagons and put up more fences?

Turning Inward

Initially, that approach felt appealing. Perhaps now was the time for the Jewish community to focus primarily on our own self-defense and interests rather than on building community with our neighbors and joining in endeavors in our larger American society. A wonderful saying in the book of Jewish wisdom known as the *Pirkei Avot* (Ethics of our Ancestors), asks the questions, "If I am not for myself, who will be for me? If I am only for myself, what am I? If not now, when?" The conventional interpretation of those questions is that we need to balance our self-interest with responsibility to others. We have to support Israel, for example, and also offer aid to impoverished communities in Haiti or West Africa. But perhaps the surge in anti-Semitism means we no longer have the luxury of devoting resources to others. Perhaps the time has come to build a higher wall around Jewish life.

I knew there was precedent for this approach. During the mid-1930s, as Hitler consolidated power in Nazi Germany and Jews were increasingly subject to economic, political, and civil restrictions, synagogue attendance surged and Jewish self-help groups proliferated. The Zionist movement, which had been unpopular in Germany because it seemed to question the patriotism of German Jews, gained adherents and financial supporters. Jews who had once shunned any connection to their Jewishness began immigrating to Israel. They became more aware of and educated about their Judaism. One of Germany's most gifted poets, Gertrude Kolmar, wrote a series of letters later collected and given the title of one of her poems: *My Gaze Is Turned Inward*. Kolmar eventually was murdered at the Auschwitz death camp.[1] Perhaps the time had come to imitate her inward gaze.

But ultimately, I thought differently. Of course I want more Jews to practice our tradition and support our institutions. But a sharp turn inward goes against my heart. Before beginning rabbinical seminary, I worked for a year at the Religious Action Center of Reform Judaism (RAC). Located in Washington, DC, the RAC brings Jewish values into public policy debates on issues such as the environment and immigration and the First Amendment. Its guiding ideal is that second question in the

Pirkei Avot. "If I am only for myself, what am I?" Working there taught me that Jewish tradition and wisdom inculcates a feeling of universal responsibility. In the Book of Genesis, God says to Abraham, "All the nations of the earth will be blessed [through you]" (22:18). To turn inward is to turn away from that calling.

In addition, turning inward feels like an act of desperation. Even with the upsurge in anti-Semitism, the United States is not 1930s Germany. For example, with a large number of marriages between Christians and Jews, Jews are more integrated into the larger culture than at any time in history. While Jews are only 1.5 percent of the US population, 58 percent of American Jews marry someone not Jewish, creating many more families with Jewish members.[2] The isolation German Jews experienced is difficult to imagine in America.

Desperation and inwardness are not the answer. Vigilance is. And so is outreach. I don't mean outreach in the sense of urging people to come to synagogue and convert to Judaism. I mean building ties with those of other faiths and sharing the wisdom of Judaism with people of all faiths. To turn outward rather than inward: that's what I have tried to do in response to the surge in anti-Semitism.

Gazing Outward

I believe this is not only pragmatic but is also an imperative taught in the Bible. It's what God asks of us, whether we are Jewish or Christian. In the Book of Numbers, Moses sends twelve leading Israelites to scout out the promised land. They are to look at the fruits and vegetables and the cities. Their reports will help shape the Israelites' military and civil plans for entering the land.

When the scouts return, they tell the people that the Canaanites cities are surrounded by imposing walls. "There are . . . powerful people who live in the land. The cities have huge fortifications" (Numbers 13:28). In other words, the Canaanites are too strong for the Israelites. Their walls are impenetrable. This seems like a bad report.

But the great medieval rabbi Rashi interpreted the verse differently. He said the scouts were correct in seeing fortified cities. They were wrong, however, to interpret them as a sign of strength. They had the right facts but derived the wrong meaning. As he wrote, "If people live in unwalled cities, they are strong and trust in their own strength. If, however, they live in fortified cities, they are weak and insecure."[3] In other words, strong people do not need high walls. Those with strength within do not need to isolate themselves from others. They can live with openness because their faith is strong.

The same is true for Jews—or any minority—today. We do not need to hide behind high walls. Openness is a sign of strength. And the ties we build with others on the outside make us even stronger. That's why, as I began to experience anti-Semitism for the first time, I did outreach. I shared Jewish wisdom and traditions with the world.

The most effective and prominent part of my outreach has been marrying couples. Between 2005 and 2012, 70 percent of non-Orthodox American Jews who married chose to marry someone who is not Jewish.[4] This percentage has grown significantly since 1970. Even the Orthodox community—which constitutes 10–15 percent of American Jewry—has seen an increase in interfaith couples. This growth indicates a drop in anti-Semitism because Jews were long seen (and saw themselves) as outsiders in a predominantly Christian America. Inmarriage was one of those walls we built. As that wall has crumbled, interfaith relationships have grown, stereotypes of Jews have changed, and anti-Semitism has weakened its hold on Americans' imaginations.

I have heard many stories similar to one told by a recent bride, who is a Polish Catholic woman married to a Jewish man. As a girl, she never really gave much thought to the stereotypical phrases she heard about Jews being cheap or rich. She certainly never thought to correct anyone about them. All that changed after she fell in love with a Jewish man. She wrote:

> At work we were talking about the holidays and a co-worker announced that he had purchased a Christmas tree that weekend, and that he got a really good deal— "Jewed him down," in fact. I stood there, growing red in the face, unsure how to respond. Then I told him that his remark was offensive to me, that it was anti-Semitic. He looked agog at me and stated that "It's an old Polish expression—not meant to do any harm." I had to tell him that it might've been an old Polish expression, but it was based on fear and hatred, and was hurtful to me.[5]

Between about 1980 and 2010, interfaith marriage reshaped American families.[6] We can see the changes when we look at pop culture. In 1964, the musical *Fiddler on the Roof* premiered. When one of the children in the story marries a Christian man, she is cut off from the family, and they mourn her decision as they would mourn a deceased child. In the 1970s, a sitcom called *Bridget Loves Bernie* featured an interfaith relationship. It was roundly lambasted by almost every Jewish religious group as a danger to Judaism and the Jewish future. Yet, by the 2000s, interfaith relationships in films and sitcoms were unremarkable. *Keeping the Faith* with Ben Stiller featured a rabbi engaged to someone not Jewish, and the *American Pie* film series featured an interfaith marriage in which the bride's old-fashioned family is charmed by Jewish rituals. Think about how many Christians you know who have a Jewish in-law (or, for that matter, parent or spouse). The more Jews people know and the more people know about Judaism, the less likely, I believe, they are to hold anti-Semitic stereotypes. (The same applies to Jews who have Christian in-laws—they have a deeper understanding of Christianity, less riddled with stereotype and suspicion than they otherwise would.)

In part because of intermarriage, American culture has become more amenable to Jewish symbols. For example, through much of the twentieth century, Jewish men would refrain from wearing a head covering in public. This skullcap—known as a *yarmulke*—symbolizes God's presence above us. It is customary to wear one during prayers in many synagogues. For Orthodox Jews, however, wearing them anywhere outside of the home is mandatory. Still, through most of the last century, Orthodox Jews would take off their yarmulkes in public. The head covering made them stand out too much. It could generate anti-Semitism.

Today, however, the yarmulke may have the opposite effect—it can invite a deeper understanding of Jewish values. I do not wear a yarmulke regularly, but I make it a practice to wear one whenever I appear on television. The first time I did so was on Fox News following the horrific school shooting in Newtown, Connecticut. It was Chanukah, and I shared that Judaism asks us to bring more light into the world, and we needed that light now more than ever. People in my congregation saw me wearing a yarmulke, and they asked me why. I said I wanted to show in public that the Jewish religious voice mattered in comforting our country at this moment. God was crying along with each of us. I was delivering this message not only as an individual but as a member of the Jewish people. The yarmulke made that clear. The following week, I received hundreds of emails, mostly from non-Jews who found comfort in my words. Some had never even heard of the holiday of Chanukah.

Does this directly reduce anti-Semitic violence? I don't know. But it does make Judaism less foreign and more real to people who may have never met someone Jewish or had exposure to Judaism.

Shut Out

In a practice beginning in the Roman Empire and continuing in many countries through the eighteenth century, Jews were legally prohibited from teaching Judaism to non-Jews;

those caught doing so could be punished by death. In addition, many Christian preachers minimized the significance of the Old Testament, and even today many people do not know that Jesus and the disciples were Jewish. So, throughout history, most Christians did not have a chance to learn about Judaism.

In addition, some Jews want to remain insular and separate from the broader community. They fear assimilation and the corruption of the culture. They prefer to live in homogenous neighborhoods and attend private schools with little interaction with the wider world. This insularity, to be sure, characterizes only a minority of the American Jewish community, but it is a strong and visible minority—and their influence is enhanced by the popular conception of the media. If you google *Jew* or *Jewish person*, the image that pops up will be a man with a beard, a black hat, and a black suit. That's the customary dress of ultra-Orthodox Jewry. This garb symbolizes a distinctive Judaism that's distant from most Jews—the clothing is a kind of high wall, a barrier that sets apart the ultra-Orthodox from everyone else.

Yet in American culture, ultra-Orthodox clothing functions as a synecdoche for Judaism more generally. In the Academy Award–winning film *Annie Hall*, a Jewish Woody Allen is sitting at a Christmas dinner with his girlfriend's Christian family in Wisconsin. He is thinking about how they see him, and he imagines they all see him with a beard and black hat. He surmises that this is their perception of any Jewish person. Woody Allen—who has done as much as anyone to introduce Judaism to American culture—can imagine that non-Jews think all Jews are different and other.

My Judaism, Reform Judaism, is much more porous than ultra-Orthodox Judaism. It prizes open windows and doors instead of high walls, and it values deep and real exchange with people of all faiths. That does not mean Reform Judaism is not a serious Judaism—rather, its openness is exactly part of what makes it meaningful.

This open-windowed Judaism strikes at the heart of one of the underlying goals of some anti-Semites, which is to diminish Jewish self-respect and make people embarrassed to be Jewish. If more people feel ashamed of their Judaism, they will be less likely to practice it, and Judaism will die. So, the best Jewish response to anti-Semitism is a prouder Judaism, not a more self-conscious and fearful one.

Avoiding fear is hard when anti-Semitic incidents make the front page of the newspapers. On January 9, 2017, for example, sixteen Jewish community centers (JCCs) in the United States received bomb threats. On January 18, ten more JCCs on the West Coast were evacuated because of bomb threats. Bewildered teachers carried out screaming two-year-olds as the buildings were evacuated. Then a major synagogue in downtown Chicago had its windows shattered, and swastikas appeared in different Jewish sites around the city. My congregation was feeling desperate. They looked to me for leadership. And I found the greatest inspiration from the students at a Jewish day school in Florida. Here's their story:

On Monday, February 17, 2017, Posnack Jewish Day School in Broward County, Florida, received a bomb threat. It came in while the older students were in the middle of their

morning prayer service. They responded as they were trained—
they retreated to the parking lot. One of the students, however,
grabbed a Torah scroll on his way out. (A Torah scroll contains
the Hebrew words of the Five Books of Moses on parchment,
and it is read ceremonially three times a week during morning
worship. A Torah scroll is considered the most sacred ritual
object in Judaism.)

Once everyone was in the parking lot, another student took
off his *tallis* (the ritual shawl one wraps around one's shoulders
during prayer) and placed it on the hood of a car. Then they
placed the Torah on top of the tallis. All the students gathered
around, and they continued to read its words, as they had been
doing when the bomb threat was called in.

These students were living in hope more than in fear.
Had they retreated to the parking lot and stood together
crying in fear and worry, we would understand. Had their
parents rushed to pick them up, we would be understandably
empathetic. But then the students' memories of Jewish learning
would be punctuated by fear and anxiety; they would imagine
living as Jews forever with a target on their collective back.
By responding with prayer and Torah, the students created a
different memory. They created a memory of community and
persistence. They combated hate with hope. That may be a
more effective response to anti-Semitism than one hundred
more video cameras or security guards.

And they inspired me to rethink what we do and
teach in my synagogue. So much of our response to anti-
Semitism was focused on more security and awareness. We
attended meetings with the Anti-Defamation League and the

Department of Homeland Security, where we learned about where to position plainclothes security officers and install thermal infrared security cameras. We taught our students and families evacuation plans. All of this is important. But after I heard the story of the students at Posnack School, we began to shift our focus to why we do what we do in synagogue. I realized parents and children were taking a risk in identifying as Jewish and practicing their Judaism. To be sure, it is not a great risk, as it has been at other times in Jewish history. Beginning in 1391 and continuing for centuries, for example, practicing Judaism in public in Spain was punishable by death or expulsion. American Jews do not face that risk. But we are still doing something that can set us apart from the majority. We are standing out, and that is always a risk. So, we need to remind ourselves of why that risk is worth taking. It is worth taking because of the Torah.

Survival by Torah

The Torah is not just a parchment—and it's not just the Five Books of Moses. The Torah symbolizes life itself, as we see evocatively in the Jewish bar and bat mitzvah services (the terms *bar mitzvah* and *bat mitzvah* denote both the coming-of-age ceremonies for thirteen-year-old boys and twelve-year-old girls as well as the persons coming of age; hence, a bat mitzvah is both the girl and the ceremony in which the community marks her mature status). In the bar or bat mitzvah service, we physically pass the Torah scroll from generation to generation. First, I give the Torah to the oldest generation present, usually the grandparents. They each take hold of the Torah and pass it to the parents. The parents then pass it to the bar or bat mitzvah. As they do so, I mention that the Torah contains the laws, teachings, values, and history of the Jewish people. Because parents and grandparents throughout history took hold of the Torah and passed it on—often through times of great persecution and uncertainty—we are blessed today to see the Torah passed into the arms of the next generation.

The Torah symbolizes Jewish survival, and it reminds us of the challenges of surviving. Without a Torah, there would be no Judaism or anti-Semitism. Torah symbolizes the truth that the world as it is falls short of the world as it ought to be. So long as this is the case, there will be anti-Semitism, and we will need to grasp and teach Torah.

The Torah contains the blueprint for Jewish life and the instructions that Jews should concern themselves with in order to be a blessing for the whole world. It contains the truth of the oneness of God and the truth that God wants people to live righteously. As the Broward County students so movingly remind us, the Torah is also a touchstone that can inspire Jews to take risks to survive. And ironically, the Torah helps explain anti-Semitism. How? Torah calls upon Jews and non-Jews to improve the world: to challenge conventions and make moral demands on others. This imperative creates tension and generates hostility. This hostility is not directed exclusively at Jews, but as the progenitor of monotheism and the people of its sourcebook, Jews are the oldest and most visible target. Reverend Edward Flannery captured this idea when he wrote, "It was Judaism that brought the concept of a God-given universal moral law into the world. . . . The Jew carries the burden of God in history [and] for this has never been forgiven."[7]

Flannery is suggesting that Jews are persecuted because we introduced a God-given moral law into the universe. The concept of moral law still generates hatred among many because it reminds us that all human power is subject to an invisible, eternal God. To be sure, Christianity and Islam spread that truth to the world in different forms, but Judaism is the source of those "burdensome moral laws" that power-hungry tyrants throughout history have resisted. Judaism brought into the world the notion of a God who is a check on human power, and much of humanity has never forgiven the Jews for doing so.

Christian Allies

Flannery's argument also explains why some Christians have been allies in fighting anti-Semitism—that is, many Christians today recognize that they share with Jews, and to some extent owe Jews a debt of gratitude for, their belief in a sovereign God. We will see in chapter 5 that certain teachings within Christianity became sources and justifications for virulent anti-Semitism. But even in the Middle Ages, bishops sometimes protected Jews from violent mobs, and several popes spoke out against the anti-Semitic charge that Jews used the blood of Christian boys to make matzah (ritual unleavened bread) during the holiday of Passover. The two most murderous anti-Semitic regimes of the twentieth century—Nazi Germany and the Soviet Union—were secular. They attacked any faith other than faith in the government and the dominant political party. Many Christians understand that an attack on Judaism is an attack on the God of humanity.

I've seen this understanding over and over again because my work on the Jewishness of Jesus has given me the opportunity to speak at many churches. In these churches, I've met Christians who have a deep desire to learn the lessons of the Hebrew Bible and to understand what Jesus and the disciples were teaching and practicing. This is not just a quest for knowledge. It is part of the building of an identity, a deeper faith.

One woman approached me after a lecture and said she wished she had been born Jewish. I was surprised because she seemed to be a devout Christian and deeply committed to her church. I asked why. She replied, "So I could live the way Jesus did." This woman's Christian faith, and her desire to be a more knowledgeable follower of Jesus, led her to an appreciation of Judaism—and that appreciation, too, can help combat anti-Semitism.

And it is important that we undertake that combating. During the same years that I have been encouraged by Christians' appreciation of Judaism, I have also increasingly seen that anti-Semitism is an urgent problem, of import for both Jews and Christians. Rising anti-Semitism points to the growing division in the world. The liberal world order, with America at its center, was created after World War II. Since then, we have lived in an era in which Jews and the world have experienced more freedom than ever before. But this freedom has begun to unravel, as we will explore more deeply in chapter

10. Anti-Semitism is one of the signs of this process. Anti-Semitism destroys societies. It lowers our moral, social, and political horizons. It dooms us to a world where the loudest and most hateful voices dominate.

The dangers we face now are epitomized in a poster I first saw in the fifth grade. My family had moved from Houston to Milwaukee. We joined a new synagogue, where I began my Hebrew studies. I was nervous the first day. I had a teacher from Israel who spoke with an accent and seemed much tougher than my teachers in Houston. I didn't know any of the other students. In this state of anxiety, I looked for a distraction.

My eyes wandered around the room and landed on a black poster with white letters. It hung on a wall near the back right-hand corner. I read its words, and they have stayed with me ever since. Looking back, I have come to see them as the impetus for this book. The words on the poster came from Reverend Martin Niemöller. He was a Lutheran pastor imprisoned in concentration camps during World War II. Initially indifferent to the rise of the Nazis, he came to strongly oppose them. Reflecting on his experience during the war, he wrote:

> First they came for the Socialists, and I did not
>   speak out—
> Because I was not a Socialist.
>
> Then they came for the Trade Unionists, and I
>   did not speak out—
> Because I was not a Trade Unionist.

> Then they came for the Jews, and I did not
>   speak out—
> Because I was not a Jew.
>
> Then they came for me—
> and there was no one left to speak out.[8]

Reverend Niemöller survived the war and became an outspoken critic of anti-Semitism and a champion for human rights. What would he say today?

Jennifer Baskerville-Burrows

Bishop, Episcopal Diocese of Indianapolis

I'd been in Indiana just one month as the new bishop-elect of the Episcopal Diocese of Indianapolis when news of the bomb threats made against our local Jewish community center came to our office. I had been to our local JCC a few days earlier to see about joining for the fitness facilities and camp programs. Reading this chapter took me back to that moment when I stood as a newcomer and ally to the Jewish community in Indianapolis.

The first part of my life was spent in Brooklyn, New York, where my brother and I were raised on knishes, corned beef, and "real" bagels. Jewish life as separate and shielded from the rest of the world was a foreign concept to our experience as African Americans coming of age in the 1970s and 1980s in New York City where we were surrounded by Jewish life and culture. Moving from Skokie, Illinois, to Indianapolis in 2017 and observing the increasingly polarized state of our nation and world has reopened my eyes to the dangerous and insidious effects of anti-Semitism and fear of "the other" not as an abstraction but as lived reality.

In times like these, when anti-Semitism, racism, and

phobias of seemingly infinite number seem to be ever present, Rabbi Moffic's reminder of the outward gaze as a biblical imperative is a word for us all. In this brief chapter, he recounts the troubled and tragic history of anti-Semitism and its roots. As a fellow optimist who struggles to make sense out of the reality in which we currently find ourselves, I find hope in the tension created by Rabbi Moffic's reading of the Torah with its imperative for Jews and non-Jews to work together to improve the world. Would that our common root in the "burdensome moral laws" that begin with Judaism and the Torah might be less a burden but a strong place to stand.

Although, as Rabbi Moffic points out, Judaism is the source of those moral laws, I believe he makes a case for a collaborative if not unified response from the three Abrahamic faiths (Judaism, Christianity, and Islam) to the end that Judaism not shoulder the brunt of the hostility caused by these moral laws alone. Indeed, I dream of a world in which none of us stands idly by in the face of anti-Semitism. Instead, we are proactive with an outward gaze to speak up for one another, build and rebuild bridges, and tear down the walls (physical, psychological, and spiritual) that separate us. This chapter affirms the case that "strong people do not need high walls." It is my hope and prayer that in our unity we might be strong together with a chorus of voices that would drown out the fear and hate.

4

The World's Oldest Hatred

If you visit Jerusalem, you will see people gathered around a wall in the center of the city. It is known as the Western Wall, and it is the only remnant of the great Jewish temple that stood in Jerusalem until the year 70 CE. In that year, the Roman armies destroyed the Temple as they fought the Jewish rebels in a war that began in 66 CE. The outer western wall of the Temple is the only part that survived, and for centuries Jews have gathered at the wall, prayed, and cried for the loss of the Temple. (Indeed, because Jews mourn the destruction of the Temple, some call this last remaining wall the Wailing Wall.)

The destruction of the Temple was part of the larger devastation experienced by the Jews during the war with the Romans. That devastation was described most clearly by a historian named Josephus. We would know very little about this period were it not for the books Josephus wrote. Christian scribes preserved these books because Josephus made several references to Jesus and to James, the brother of Jesus. But Josephus himself was not a follower of Jesus. He was a Jew born in Jerusalem. He became a governor and military commander. When his brigade was defeated, he switched sides and became an advisor to the Roman army. He eventually became an official scribe for the emperor. Despite seeming to betray the Jewish army, Josephus never left Judaism. His first books, *The Jewish Wars* and *Jewish Antiquities*, teach us much about Jewish practices and culture during the first centuries. But the book helping us pinpoint the origins of anti-Semitism is his final book, *Against Apion*.

The First Anti-Semite

In *Against Apion*, Josephus refers to an Egyptian priest from the third century BCE named Manetho. Manetho wrote a history of Egypt under the rule of the Pharaohs. Even today his work is a valuable guide to ancient Egypt. But what makes Manetho the first prominent anti-Semite is that he offers a very different version of the Exodus story than we find in the Bible. His version establishes Jews as a deceitful people dedicated to undermining society wherever they live.

According to Manetho, Jews are a combination of two peoples—shepherds who invaded Egypt and lepers who were driven out of Egypt by Pharaoh. The shepherds invaded Egypt from the north (which would be modern-day Israel) sometime during the seventeenth century BCE. They succeeded in conquering Egypt and ruling them with oppressive laws until they were driven out after about a hundred years.

Then, after native Egyptians retook control, a terrible plague infected the land. Pharaoh received a dream in which he was told to isolate the sick lepers and imprison them in the "deserted city of the shepherds." In that city, however, the lepers came under the influence of a renegade Egyptian priest who proclaimed a belief in one God and rejected the traditional Egyptian gods. This priest went to Jerusalem, where he made an alliance with the shepherds who had fled there. Together these two groups united and conquered Egypt. They made the lives of the Egyptians miserable, setting fires to their cities and destroying their sacrifices. They forced the Egyptian priests and prophets to sacrifice animals sacred to them and stripped these leaders of their titles and honor. Eventually, however, the Egyptians revolted and drove out the shepherd-lepers. These shepherd-lepers are the Jews, the people of Israel, because that is the land to which they fled after both expulsions from Egypt.

Manetho's account proved influential and enduring. It established the Jews as impure and impious. They were lepers who had destroyed all of Egypt's gods. They were also brutal and tyrannical, as evidenced in the way they subjugated native Egyptians. They are a mortal threat to all other peoples. Writing in 2014, Professor David Nirenberg concluded that Manetho's views "proved so useful that they continue to provide cornerstones for ideologies up to the present day."[1] Manetho's accounts and influence make him the first prominent anti-Semite.

Why Then?

This fact may be interesting, but the pressing question for those of us struggling with the rise of anti-Semitism today is why Manetho's account emerged when it did. What was it about the ancient Near East that provided a fertile context for anti-Semitism? Two critical explanations stand out. The first is assimilation. By the third century BCE, Jews were adopting much of the Hellenistic culture. They lived in cities, spoke Greek, traded, and took on Greek names. The extent to which they assimilated Greek culture can be seen in the first major translation of the Hebrew Bible into another language. In the third century BCE, the Bible was translated into Greek—today, we refer to that translation as the Septuagint. Manetho's rewriting of the Exodus story may have been sparked by this translation because the biblical Exodus was now accessible to the Greek-speaking public. But the creation of the Septuagint is also important for understanding assimilation because it suggests that some Jews could not read the Bible in Hebrew. They could only read it in Greek. However, Jews did not assimilate fully. They maintained a belief in one God and continued to eat certain foods and pray in particular synagogues.

This meant that Jews were both part of and apart from the wider culture—which created tension because it suggested to other groups who had adopted Hellenism more fully that the Jews thought of themselves as somehow unique and superior. The notion of cultural pluralism we have today did not exist in the third century. The pressures to conform to the culture of the ruling power was immense. When Jews resisted it, they became targets.

This was the first time in history that Jews had had the opportunity or incentive to resist the larger culture. Until 586 BCE, Jews had lived in their own independent state, save for the time in Egypt, in which they were forcibly segregated. Even after 586 BCE, when the Babylonians conquered Judea, Jews were able to maintain a strong form of political independence under Persian rule and even rebuilt the Temple that had been destroyed by the Babylonians.

After Alexander the Great conquered the Persian Empire and spread Hellenistic culture, however, pressure to conform increased. Jews were caught between two worlds: the Hellenistic world, which lauded the body and athletics and the pantheon of Greek gods, and the spiritual world of the Hebrew Bible. Jews struggled to remain in both. Their commitment to staying Jewish and not adopting the Greek gods led to hostility, of which Manetho's anti-Semitic tract was the most enduring and influential example.

The Deeper Reasons

Even so, Jewish commitment to maintaining their separate identity does not fully explain the origins and rise of anti-Semitism. There were certainly other groups that tried to remain distinct. Only Jews, however, sparked an enduring hatred. Why? The answer lies in specific Jewish beliefs that were noxious to the wider culture. Some of these beliefs generate hostility to this day.

The first is the Jewish understanding of God. Jews believe that God is invisible. God is incorporeal. God cannot be seen but can be heard through the words of Torah and the Prophets. A famous Jewish legend imagines the first Jew—Abraham—seeing several idols who were worshipped as gods. He recognizes the foolishness of this approach, and then he smashes all the idols except the biggest one. He puts his club in the arms of the biggest one, and then tells his father that idol smashed all the other ones. The lesson, of course, is that the idols have no such power. Only the God we cannot see is the sovereign of the universe.

By seeing only one God in the universe, Judaism denies the legitimacy of other gods. This angered their neighbors. As one scholar has put it, "No other nation at that time denied the gods of its neighbors. . . . None of the peoples refrained from partaking of the sacrifices offered to the gods, except the Jews. None of the peoples refused to send gifts to its neighbors' temples, except the Jews."[2] Jews, it seems, did not play well in the divine sandbox of the ancient Near East.

Relatedly, Jews believe that God has chosen the Jews to be God's messenger to humanity. That is why God asked them to receive the Torah and follow a special set of laws given by God at Mount Sinai. Jews would be, according to the Book of Exodus, God's "most precious possession" (19:5). It is easy to see why this self-understanding could lead to hostility. Claiming to be chosen by God for a special mission seems to imply a superiority. God, it suggests, chose the Jews over everyone else. God gave the Jews a special love greater than all others. This view was accentuated by Jewish dietary practices and other elements that tended to keep them separate from other peoples. When the Bible was translated into Greek for the first time, others became aware of this Jewish self-understanding, which likely fueled anti-Semitism.

But this idea of being a chosen people does not imply superiority. It need not have led to anti-Semitism because it was a Jewish self-perception—not a statement of absolute truth about the universe. The Bible makes clear several times that the Jewish people were not chosen because of some inherent quality. Every person is equal before God. Rather, Jews were chosen to keep up a set of obligations that requires affirmation and continual self-examination. Chosenness describes a relationship between one group and God; it does not describe a hierarchy among various groups of people. For example, if you are married, you may see your spouse as your chosen partner. He or she has a unique claim on your love. That does not mean your relationship is superior to every other relationship. It simply means that in your self-understanding, your spouse is beloved by you in a unique way, as you are by him or her. The same is true in the relationship between Jews and God. (In fact, the metaphor of marriage is used in both the Bible and in Jewish commentary on the Bible to describe the relationship between God and the Jewish people.) Even so, non-Jews' responses to the concept of Jewish chosenness continue to drive anti-Semitism. The claim that Jews see themselves as superior to others has persisted from the time of Manetho through today.

Chosenness has not only been a source of anti-Semitism; it has also caused great internal struggle for me. Since I was called to be a rabbi, I have struggled with the idea of chosenness. This Jewish belief seemed to conflict with my core values, especially my identity as an American. I studied American history in college and considered pursuing a doctorate and becoming a professor. The overriding thrust of American history is toward equality. We emphasize what unites us over what divides us. Even with our embrace of multiculturalism, the idea of the melting pot persists. Each generation of immigrants to America loses some of their unique cultural attributes and adopts and adapts some of the new cultural forms they find here. In this context, being a chosen people feels out of place. Why would Jews want to identify as the chosen people and set ourselves apart from others? Why create another barrier when America is built on the idea of boundlessness? If we are so concerned about anti-Semitism, why emphasize our difference from the rest of the world?

In answering this question, I came first to a seemingly obvious truth, a truth I often forget: Each of us is different. No human beings are exactly the same. A Jewish legend compares God to a coin maker, but then points out an essential difference. When a coin maker mints coins, they all come out the same. When God creates human beings, they all come out different. Figuring out what makes us unique—nurturing our own character and skills—is part of growing up. What makes us different is essential to who we are.

Understanding ourselves as having unique responsibilities and practices is part of being Jewish. Most religious groups, it seems, see themselves as different in one way or another. Christians are saved through the death and resurrection of

Jesus. Muslims are obliged to follow the words of the Koran. These practices set us apart. Difference—being chosen to follow a certain path—is what has allowed each faith group to survive over thousands of years.

Always Different

What made Jews uniquely susceptible to ongoing hatred is that they always remained different from the surrounding culture in which they lived. Christianity became the dominant culture in the Western world when the Roman emperor Constantine converted to Christianity. Christianity became the religion of the empire, while Jews remained different and set apart. When Muhammad conquered the Middle East in the seventh century, Jews remained different and apart. When Moses's first son was born, he named him Gershom, which means "stranger there," because Moses saw himself as "a stranger in a strange land" (Exodus 2:22 KJV). That description fit the Jewish people over time. They were seen as a strange people with strange practices, and to survive, they maintained those practices and saw them as part of being God's chosen people. So, chosenness was a strategy for survival and service to God, not a state of superiority.

Rabbi Jonathan Sacks, the former chief rabbi of Great Britain, has helped me see the idea of chosenness as a way of combating anti-Semitism and hatred without erasing what makes us unique. Difference is a divine gift, not a condition to overcome. Those who seek to erase Jews' differences go against God's desire. God, says Sacks, "chooses Israel, the people who are called to be different, to show that for God, difference matters. . . . They were strangers to teach that God loves the stranger. They were different, yet God set on them His love, to teach the dignity of difference."[3] With all due respect to John Lennon, I believe a brotherhood of man cannot exist without religion. A true brotherhood is one where we live our particular religion and honor the deepest beliefs of others.

Jews carry that message to the world. Chosenness serves a universal purpose. When we maintain our differences—when Jews continue to display a commitment to unique practices and beliefs—we illustrate God's love for all of creation. God does not want people to believe all the same things and follow the exact same laws. Yes, there are core moral truths binding all people. In Judaism, we call those the Noahide commandments—you shall not murder, steal, and so forth. But God created us differently, with varied beliefs and practices. If God wanted us to live in the exact same way, God would have made us in that way.

This is not just an idealistic belief. It has real consequences. When we believe God values differences, we refuse to condone persecution in the name of a higher power. If we reject the idea that people need to assimilate and follow one particular culture or set of beliefs, persecution of the other loses its ideological justification, and we come to see that we should honor those who are different because God (or nature, for those of no or a different faith) made them that way. It is much easier to hate and hurt someone when you believe you are doing it for a good reason. Human beings, as Sigmund Freud understood, may have an aggressive instinct. But we are more likely to deploy that instinct to hurt others when we have some intellectual or religious justification. Understanding God as desiring differences among people takes away the reason so many have offered for persecuting others.

More at Stake

Chosenness was not the only target of non-Jews' ire. So was the Sabbath. Ancient Greek and Roman writings charged Jews with laziness because Jews rested for a full day. This laziness was a sign of their unworthiness as a people. According to such writings, the Sabbath was a celebration of slothfulness and weakness. Some Roman writers even claimed that Jerusalem was conquered and taken from the Jews because they refused to fight on the Sabbath.[4]

Reading these Greek and Roman writers carefully has convinced me that more is at stake here than a simple charge of laziness. The Sabbath symbolizes a deep division between Jews and Hellenistic culture. Whereas the Hellenistic ideal was the physically adroit man of action, the Jewish ideal was a family enjoying the pleasures of companionship and study. The Sabbath was a day to experience that ideal world. The Sabbath is a time for a family meal, for prayer at the synagogue and for study of the Torah. It encompasses several of the core practices—eating and prayer—that distinguish Jews from others. In short, on the Sabbath, Jews lived in their own world, separate and apart from others. It was a consistent weekly reminder of Jewish difference and community.

Jews also believe that the Sabbath—which focuses on rest,

study, physical intimacy (for married couples), and *shalom bayit* (peace in the home)—is a taste of heaven on earth. In depicting the world as it could be if we all followed God's commandments, the Sabbath is a weekly reminder that the world is not yet what it could be. It at once implicitly criticizes our current social and economic arrangements and holds out the possibility of a better world. This emphasis on the possibility of a better world means Judaism takes a linear view of time. Progress is possible. We can improve, change, and grow. If we do so, we will eventually reach a messianic age, a time of perfection, symbolized by the Sabbath.

This linear view of time stands at odds with the Hellenistic view of time. The Hellenistic perspective was that time is like the seasons. It repeats over and over. Our fate is sealed. The fickle gods have determined our futures for us, and we cannot change those divine plans no matter how hard we try: to pretend otherwise is to invite catastrophe (remember the story of Oedipus Rex).

The Jewish view of time, as symbolized in the Sabbath, so troubled the Greeks that they had to mistranslate a biblical verse when they produced the Septuagint, the first Greek translation of the Bible. In the Torah, Genesis 2 says, "On the seventh day God completed the work He had made." We know that on the *seventh* day, God *rested*. Rest completed the work of creation. The idea that God completed work while resting was incomprehensible to the Greeks. Rest is rest. Work is work. Yet, completing the world required work. Therefore, God could not both rest and complete the work of creation on the seventh day. So, the Septuagint translation of Genesis 2:2

reads, "On the sixth day God completed His work." This small change was made to harmonize Genesis with Hellenistic views about time, rest, and work.

The ideals of the Sabbath also captured another core division between the two groups. Central to the Greek worldview is hierarchy and power. The word *politics* comes from *polis*, the Greek word for city-state. Politics is the distribution of power, and it depends on hierarchies. As the greatest Greek philosopher, Plato, wrote, the ideal society was one in which the philosopher-king held power and rule over the commoner. Slavery was an accepted part of the natural, divinely ordained order of Greek life. God created slaves to serve their masters.

The Sabbath is fundamentally at odds with this Hellenistic view of the universe. On Shabbat (the Jewish Sabbath), people are bound by neither work nor divine whim. On Shabbat, there is no master and slave: everyone, including animals, rests before God. On Shabbat, we are simply part of creation, and we receive a vision of ultimate goodness and peace—the world as it should be. Sustaining that vision through weekly Sabbath observance (and, when we can, drawing shades of Sabbath ideals into the week) is part of Jewish life. Manetho was offended by this vision and wrote the first anti-Semitic tract in response to it.

Is It Anti-Semitism?

One of the challenges in assessing the origins of anti-Semitism is distinguishing normal political and ethnic conflict from a unique hostility toward Jews. Groups in the ancient Near East fought constantly with each other. Even today countries compete for power and influence. What makes it reasonable to speak of hostility toward the Jews as something unique?

A partial answer is the persistent trope of Jews as subhuman, a people inherently inferior to other human beings by dint of their origins and way of life. When Manetho says the Jews are descended from lepers, he is dehumanizing them. When the Greek philosopher Philostratus claimed that Jewish practices separate Jews from humanity altogether—Jews "have long been in revolt . . . against humanity; and a race that has made its own a life apart and irreconcilable, that cannot share with the rest of mankind in the pleasures of the table nor join in their libations or prayers or sacrifices"[5]—he created a template for future anti-Semitic charges. His words, written more than two thousand years ago, suggest Jews are cut off from other human beings, making their persecution more easily justified. Once you see Jews "in revolt . . . against humanity," it is easy to see Jews as unworthy of sharing in the common life and dignity of human society.

I am powerfully reminded of the significance of dehumanization whenever I tour the Holocaust Museum in Washington, DC. I take a group of students there every year, and one room always evokes the deepest response. It is a room re-creating a town from Poland. It tells the history of the Jewish community of the town over hundreds of years and includes thousands of pictures of people engaged in daily life—eating family meals, visiting the shoe shop, sitting and talking on a park bench. This community's vibrant life was utterly destroyed by an ideology that did not see Polish Jews as truly human.

The exhibit at the Holocaust Museum shows the ultimate physical consequences of dehumanization: an entire village was murdered. But dehumanization happens in less extreme ways as well. One form of dehumanizing is to assign motives and values to a person based on one part of his or her identity. Manetho saw Jews not as individuals but as *The* Jews, a self-interested group who only think of gaining power and oppressing others. David Nirenberg describes his overall view as "Mosaic misanthropy."[6] Even though Manetho knew only one Jewish community—the one in Alexandria—and the majority of Jews lived elsewhere, he claimed to know the real motives of all Jews. When we assign motives and views to an individual purely on the basis of that person's ethnic or religious identity, we are dehumanizing him or her.

Manetho dehumanized Jews as a group, and when you dehumanize a group, it becomes easier to make any number of specific charges stick to that group. We will see that throughout subsequent chapters. But we also see it in the world today. There is no consistency or underlying pattern to the range of justifications given for anti-Semitism. A remarkable observation from a Polish literary critic, Konstanty Jeleński, captures the conflicting tropes and beliefs of anti-Semites. As Jeleński wrote in 1968:

> Poles have never come out against Jews "because they are Jews" but because Jews are dirty, greedy, mendacious, because they wear earlocks, speak jargon, do not want

to assimilate, and *also* because they *do* assimilate, cease using their jargon, are nattily dressed, and want to be regarded as Poles. Because they lack culture and because they are overly cultured. Because they are superstitious, backward and ignorant, and because they are damnably capable, progressive and ambitious. Because they have long, hooked noses, and because it is sometimes difficult to distinguish them from "pure Poles." ... Because they are bankers and capitalists and because they are Communists and agitators.[7]

As we can see, justifications for anti-Semitism frequently contradict each other. Jews can be made to fit whatever ideology a particular person or group hates.

Lasting Influence

Manetho's accusation that Jews were lepers exiled from Egypt changed how many viewed the Jews as a people. Manetho was the first to portray Jews as "the other," as a group with deceptive motives—and that notion has underpinned anti-Semitic fantasies about Jews ever since.

In the generations after Manetho wrote, his ideas were picked up by Romans, and Jews suffered under Roman rule. Then, several centuries after Manetho wrote, a new religion was born. As that religion grew, Manetho's ideas took on a new and dangerous form.

5

The Devil and the Jews

Christianity Through the Ages

arly in my career, a couple came to me to officiate at their
wedding. He was Catholic and she was Jewish. That is
not unusual. Almost 70 percent of non-Orthodox Jews in the
United States marry someone who is not Jewish.[1] What was
more unusual, however, was their request that a priest officiate
alongside me.

My initial thought was no. A Jewish wedding was a Jewish
service. I wouldn't ask a priest if I could be part of a Catholic
service. So why change the nature of a Jewish wedding service?
I worried that a joint service would convey confusion. The
couple, some might conclude, has not decided what they want
to do about religion. They want to avoid making a tough
decision and keep their options open. That did not seem like a
viewpoint I should encourage.

But my conversations with the couple and with one of my

mentors led me to say yes to the request. Both faiths were a big part of the couple's lives, and it became clear to me that they weren't avoiding an important choice—rather, they were seeking to honor who they both were as people. Who was I to deny the Catholic groom a representative from his heritage, especially if his bride was comfortable with it?

As we began planning the wedding, the bride's family made a specific request of me. "Can you make sure," they asked, "that the priest does not mention Jesus at all during the ceremony?" Part of me was angry at the bride's parents. Why should I tell a priest what he can and cannot say? I would not want a priest telling me such things. But another part of me understood the feeling behind their wish.

For many Jews, especially those who grew up in the shadow of the Holocaust, Jesus symbolizes anti-Semitism. He symbolizes a church and belief system that harbored anti-Semitic views and promoted vicious attacks against Jews. Most Christians I know do not see Jesus in this way. For many Jews, however, the association persists, and these parents did not want to feel the ambivalence and discomfort they knew they'd feel if they heard the name "Jesus" during their daughter's wedding.

I explained this to the groom, who talked about it with his priest. The priest agreed to honor the bride's parents' request. And then he did something else wonderful. He invited me to speak to the church about the history of anti-Semitism within the church. To prepare my remarks, I had to learn more than the vague things I knew about the extent to which Christianity has been harnessed to, and indeed has produced, anti-Semitism. It was uncomfortable and sometimes upsetting to learn that history. At the same time, the very undertaking—learning this painful history exactly so that I could grow in friendship with a Christian congregation that wished to confront its tradition's complicity with the sin of anti-Semitism—was itself a step away from Christian anti-Semitism and toward healing.

The Beginning

The first Christians saw themselves as authentic Jews who had experienced and learned from the birth, death, and resurrection of the Jewish Messiah. They believed they were living out the authentic message of the God of Israel, who had come to earth in human form. They saw this truth revealed in the Hebrew Bible and confirmed by the testimony of eyewitnesses.

Over several decades, these Jewish devotees of Jesus became increasingly isolated from other groups within the Jewish community, who did not see Jesus as meeting the requirements of the Messiah. The Messiah was supposed to bring about peace and Israelite independence. The Jewish wars with the Romans between 66 and 70 CE seemed to make those requirements impossible to meet. In addition, some Jewish followers of Jesus began to preach their message to Gentiles throughout the Roman Empire. They decided that Gentiles need not, in order to join the community of Jesus-followers, convert to Judaism, adopt male circumcision, and follow the dietary laws. These decisions further divided Jesus-followers from other parts of the Jewish community. In time, the followers of Jesus who were not born Jewish outnumbered those who had come from the Jewish community, and the group became a separate religion.

Scholars do not know when this process was complete; it likely unfolded over several generations, even centuries. But by the Council of Nicaea in 325 CE (a gathering of bishops and other church leaders to hammer out certain aspects of Christian doctrine), the split between Judaism and Christianity was clear, and certain anti-Jewish beliefs within Christianity crystallized. These beliefs had horrific consequences. And a few of them persist today.

In this chapter, we will begin by asking: What specific views of Jews shaped early Christianity? Why did theologians arrive at those particular views? Then we will examine the consequences of these beliefs. We will see how Jewish suffering resulted directly from certain Christian Scriptures, practices, movements, and leaders. And we'll note that while many of the violent expressions of Christian anti-Semitism have diminished, some anti-Semitic theological views persist in both overt and subtle ways.

Theology

One of the most consequential anti-Semitic Christian teachings has been the idea that Jews killed Jesus—an idea that threads through the history of Christian speech about Jesus and that, according to one recent study, 26 percent of Americans believe today.[2] Where does this belief come from?

Central to the New Testament's four Gospels are accounts of the death and resurrection of Jesus. Culpability for his death would seem to rest with Pontius Pilate. Crucifixion was a Roman punishment, and as governor of Judea, he would have issued any death sentence. Yet, the Gospels suggest Jewish priests and the Sanhedrin shared some responsibility. They pushed Pilate into killing Jesus. The Gospel of Matthew, as we will see, suggests Pilate was forced by the Jews to inflict a punishment he did not really want to give.

This idea that Jews are responsible for the death of Jesus—who himself was Jewish—became known as "deicide," the charge of having killed (-cide, as in *homicide*) God (*deus*). The biblical text perhaps most frequently held up in support of this is Matthew 27:24-25: "Pilate saw that he was getting nowhere and that a riot was starting. So he took water and washed his hands in front of the crowd. 'I'm innocent of this man's blood,' he said. 'It's your problem.' All the people replied, 'Let his blood be on us and on our children.' "

The last sentence in particular stands out. "All the people" are a group of Jews witnessing Jesus's execution. They seem to accept responsibility and suggest that responsibility extends to their children as well. One can read this verse as the text by which Jews become responsible for killing Jesus, even though it was, of course, Romans who killed Jesus—and because Matthew says that Jesus's blood is on the Jews then present "and our children," the guilt for Jesus's death—his blood—is on the Jews of the first century and their descendants for all time.

Not all Christians throughout history interpreted this

verse this way. Some theologians say the speakers symbolize all of sinful humanity. But many early church fathers and later theologians, such as Augustine and Martin Luther, did see this verse as an indictment of the Jews: Jews caused the death of God. Numerous other biblical verses suggest Jewish responsibility for Jesus's death. Matthew, however, is most significant because it directly assigns blame to future generations of Jews as well. The consequences of this interpretation of the verse have been horrific. Before looking at those consequences, however, we will look at two other influential theological claims.

Supersessionism

The second claim is known as *supersessionism* or *replacement theology*, mentioned briefly in chapter 2. Supersessionism is the idea that the church and Christians have "superseded" and replaced Jews and Judaism as God's covenantal partner. In this view, God has removed his favor from the followers of the laws of the Torah and bestowed his favor instead upon followers of Jesus.

The superseded old covenant rested on Abraham's circumcision and the giving of the Law at Mount Sinai. It has been replaced by the new covenant, marked by belief in the death and resurrection of Jesus. The new Israel—those who believe Jesus is Christ—has replaced the old Israel as God's chosen people. The new covenant is also superior to the old because it is open to all, not only those who practice Judaism, and it is marked by the spirit and not the flesh.

The Book of Hebrews articulates this view clearly: "When it says new, it makes the first obsolete. And if something is old and outdated, it's close to disappearing" (8:13). Many scholars suggest the destruction of the Jerusalem temple by the Romans in 70 CE lent credibility to the supersessionist thesis because it illustrated that God's favor and protection had left the Jewish temple and the Jewish people. Professor and columnist James Carroll, for example, argues that the destruction of the Temple was the moment when followers of Jesus separated from the Jewish people and began to form a full-fledged religion. The Temple's destruction was a watershed moment, marking the end of the old covenant and the beginning of the new.[3]

Just Deserts

A third, related, charge Christians have often made against Jews is that Jews suffer and warrant punishment because of their rejection of Jesus. The Jews refused to accept the new covenant. They persecuted one of their own who delivered God's message first to them. Therefore, their suffering—first signaled by the destruction of the Temple—is God's ongoing punishment, and it is evidence for the truth of Christianity.

The most articulate and influential proponent of this view is Saint Augustine of Hippo. His theology deeply shaped the Western church—it is to Augustine, for example, that the church owes the doctrine of heritable original sin.

Augustine's thinking about Jews was also influential. Emphasizing Jewish responsibility for the death of Jesus,

Augustine argued that Pilate wanted to save Jesus, but he gave in to the insistence of the Jews, who truly believed Jesus had blasphemed God by claiming he was the Son of God. The Jews did not understand who Jesus was, and, feeling threatened by his growing power, they had him killed.

Augustine then tried to explain why God did not destroy the Jews altogether in punishment for their act of deicide. He concluded that the survival of the Jews is part of God's ongoing plan to teach the truth of Christianity. The Jews, he said, are and will be preserved because they make evident to the world that the promises Christianity fulfills are ancient and not simply invented by Christians. Their suffering and scattering around the world demonstrate the consequences of blindness to God's truth. And although their crime of deicide, Augustine said, justifies their murder, God's mercy prevails, and their existence reminds Christians of the consequences of disobedience.

The Crusades

Beliefs about supersessionism and deicide were just that—beliefs. But Christian history has also been riddled with actual violence done by Christians to Jews (often, though not always, in the name of deicide charges). This section is a difficult one because we will review several of the most persistent Christian expressions of anti-Semitism with an eye toward understanding how thoroughly the fabric of Christianity has been shot through with violent fantasies about Jews and how often those fantasies have enabled actual violence. We will encounter some upsetting truths. But they will help us understand how important battling anti-Semitism—and, specifically, Christian anti-Semitism—is today.

Prior to the Holocaust in the twentieth century, the most horrific period of Jewish persecution was the Crusades. In 1096, Pope Urban II issued a call for Christians to reclaim the Holy Land from the Muslims (who had conquered the land in 1071). This call led to a series of organized journeys to Palestine, with the first one beginning in 1096 and the second in 1147. In 1096, between twenty thousand and thirty thousand Christians responded to the pope's call and set off from western Europe on horseback and in groups. On the way, they marched through dozens of Jewish towns.

While Pope Urban II targeted Muslims, the crusaders committed themselves to destroying infidels more generally. They were fighting a war for Christ, and anyone deemed against Christ was the enemy. As historian Leon Poliakov noted, the crusaders "were God's avengers, appointed to punish all infidels, whoever they might be. . . . What could be more natural than to take revenge along the way upon the various infidels living in Christian territories?"[4] Jews were the first and most frequent infidels crusaders saw along the way. Between 1096 and 1099, tens of thousands of Jews in the Rhineland were murdered; entire Jewish sections of towns were destroyed.

The attacks on Jews were often not directly by the crusaders. Crusaders' calls for Christian victory ignited passions in hundreds of local villages. Dozens of accounts exist of ordinary villagers entering synagogues and surrounding streets inhabited by Jews. Sometimes bishops would try to stop the mobs from attacking the Jewish quarter. But they were usually unable to do so, and over the eleventh and twelfth centuries, thousands of Jews were killed. Indeed, the murder of Jews became a self-perpetuating loop, suggesting to Christians that God's patience with these infidels had run out, thus feeding yet more violence.

In contrast to the First Crusade, the Second Crusade began with harsh anti-Jewish intentions. In 1147, as it broke out, a prominent French cleric proclaimed, "What is the good of going to the end of the world, at great loss of men and money, to fight the Saracens, when we permit among us other infidels a thousand times more guilty towards Christ than the Mohammedans?"[5] While the First Crusade decimated the Jewish community of the Rhineland, the Second Crusade destroyed Jewish France.

Almost two hundred years later, in 1320, Spain became the target of the Third Crusade, also known as the Shepherds' Crusade. A shepherd from Normandy raised an army seeking to drive Muslims out of Spain. As they marched south, they attacked Jews in major French cities and eventually entered Spain, where they murdered about three hundred Jews before the Spanish king succeeded in stopping them. The king and royal officials relied on Spanish Jews for major government and economic roles, and they fined communities where local officials had supported the Shepherds' army.

Despite its failure, the Shepherds' Crusade ignited more popular anti-Jewish feeling in Europe. Over time government and church officials lost the ability or the will to prevent mob hysteria, and Jews were expelled from England (1290), France (1394), Spain (1492), and various regions of Germany, Italy, and the Balkan Peninsula between 1200 and 1600. Christopher Columbus's ship left three days later than scheduled in August 1492, in part because the harbor was clogged with ships of Jews leaving Spain.

In addition to the number of Jews killed, an important consequence of the Crusades was the blurring of the line between mob action and official, church-sanctioned policies. While prominent bishops and even popes condemned the murder of Jews, virtually none of the murderers were punished, and many bishops simply looked on as their Jewish communities were destroyed. This fuzzy line between authority and mass hysteria appears and reappears in the violent history of anti-Semitism: legal authorities were complicit in the pogroms (murderous attacks of Jews) in Russia and the Ukraine in the late nineteenth century, and even in the 1913 lynching of Leo Frank in Atlanta.

Leo Frank was a Jew from New York who had married into an Atlanta Jewish family who owned a pencil factory. He managed the factory when an employee, thirteen-year-old Mary Phagan, was murdered there. Authorities accused Frank, even though the evidence was minimal and actually pointed to the factory's custodian. Frank was found guilty and sentenced to death for the crime. Appeals to the governor, however, resulted in his death sentence being commuted to life in prison. But locals from Phagan's hometown of Marietta did not accept this as justice and kidnapped Frank from prison. They drove him back to Marietta and hanged him from an oak tree. Accounts of the Leo Frank murder point out that among those who organized the prison break and hanging were prominent citizens, including "a judge, a sheriff, a mayor, incumbent and former state legislators, and a former governor of Georgia."[6]

Jews and the Devil

Christian violence against Jews did not occur in a vacuum. It embedded itself within Christian practices. Indeed, inseparable from many acts of violence was a long history of Christians speaking about or visually depicting Jews as a violent "other." For example, in the Middle Ages, meditating on the crucifixion was important to many Christians' piety. In the prayerful meditations Christians used as a devotional aid and the theatrical renditions of the passion play many gathered to watch, Jews were depicted in horrible terms—as enacting unspeakable violence upon Jesus as he walked to his death, and as relishing the violence.

Christian preaching and art also portrayed Jews in league with the devil. John 8:44, for example, reads, "Your father is the devil. You are his children, and you want to do what your father wants. He was a murderer from the beginning. He has never stood for the truth, because there's no truth in him. Whenever that liar speaks, he speaks according to his own nature, because he's a liar and the father of liars." This equation of the Jews with the devil solves an important theological question: who was wicked enough to murder God? Only the devil. Therefore, Jews are the devil incarnate. The charge appeared prominently in the writings of the fourth-century church father John Chrysostom, who denounced from the pulpit Christians who still observed Jewish feasts and festivals. According to his writing, many followers of Jesus still gathered in synagogues and observed the Sabbath and heard the sound of the shofar during the Jewish New Year. They were, he said, engaging in demonic rituals. In a series of sermons he gave in Antioch, Chrysostom said the Jews "sacrificed their sons and daughters to devils: they outraged nature; and overthrew from their foundations the laws of relationship. They are become worse than the wild beasts, and for no reason at all, with their own hands they murder their own offspring, to worship the avenging devils who are the foes of our life." In the same sermon series, he said Jews rejoice in Jesus's death, and are "fit for slaughter."[7] Reading his words in the aftermath of the Holocaust—where six million Jews were slaughtered—is chilling.

The portrayal of devilish Jews intensified in the Middle Ages. Before then, artistic portrayals of Jews tended to show them simply as witnesses to the crucifixion. But in the mid-twelfth century, art changed, and Jews became "the most powerful and poisonous symbol in all of Christian art."[8] Hundreds of works of art appeared, each depicting Jews with bulging eyes and horns. A famous depiction of the crucifixion by Peter Lombard from 1166 shows a devilish Jew standing next to the crucified Jesus and spearing him. In addition, as historian Sara Lipton points out, "The Jews' affiliation with the devil might be signaled by placing him in hell, perching a demon on his shoulder, giving him subtle beast-like features, wrapping a snake around his eyes . . . and depicting him with a goatee, tail, and/or horns."⁹ Some of this imagery has been carried into the modern world, especially in anti-Semitic portrayal of Israeli political leaders. A report by the Anti-Defamation League found numerous examples in mainstream Arab and Egyptian newspapers of Israel's prime minister, Benjamin Netanyahu, with devil's horns.

Ritual Murder

By depicting Jews as the devil incarnate or as children of the devil, medieval theologians and artists highlighted their extreme wickedness. Christian writing charged Jews with crimes so outrageous that they often feel lifted from the script of a horror film. The most famous and persistent charge is that Jews murder Christian children and use their blood for religious rituals. That charge first emerged in 1114 in the English town of Norwich, when a twelve-year-old boy named William went missing. William was known to have frequent contact with the Jewish community because he was an apprentice to a tanner of hides who dealt frequently with Jews.

Five years after the boy disappeared, a Benedictine monk named Thomas Monmouth arrived in Norwich. He claimed he was investigating and writing a story about what happened to the missing boy. He did, and he published it as *The Life and Miracles of Saint William of Norwich*. No corroborating evidence exists for his account, but it spread across Europe and led to many unsolved child murders being attributed to Jews in subsequent decades.

According to Monmouth, a Jew deceived William's mother into letting him come to work for a few days with the "archdeacon" by giving her three shillings. This figure of three shillings echoes the thirty pieces of silver the Romans gave Judas to betray Jesus. In truth, says Monmouth's account, William was not going to work. He was brought into a Jew's home and tortured for three days. He suffered and was murdered in a way similar to Jesus. They shaved his head and stabbed it with thorn points. They pulled his body in painful directions with tight knots. He was finally murdered on the first day of Passover, which was the Wednesday of Holy Week. William's body was discovered on the weekend of Easter, and he was buried on the following Tuesday.

The details Monmouth provided about the tortures William of Norwich underwent were not superfluous. They were part and parcel of medieval Christians' interest in the intense suffering Jesus experienced on the cross. Contemplating the suffering of Christ in great detail became a more widespread Christian practice, and art depicting the extraordinary physical pain Jesus underwent became more commonplace. Through prayer and acts of piety, Christians were meant to imaginatively connect to Jesus's own experience. Monmouth's details of the child's suffering evoked that experience. That led his book to receive more attention and enhanced the image of William as a Jesus-like figure who suffered a tragic death at the hands of the Jews.

In addition to the parallels with Jesus, Monmouth wanted to send a message about Jewish wickedness in the way he told the story: William's murder was the fulfillment of the Jewish community's annual practice of selecting one Christian child to murder during Passover. That child's blood would be used to make matzah (unleavened bread) for Passover. This accusation became known as the *blood libel*. According to Monmouth, the leaders of world Jewry gathered together every year to decide which Jewish community would have to perform a ritual murder that year. This ritual murder was a mandatory reenactment of their murder of Jesus. It served to avenge the suffering they had endured as a result of that murder. Monmouth claimed he received secret, insider information about this custom from Christians who had converted from Judaism.

Monmouth's book spawned many imitators. Before the end of the twelfth century, the ritual murder charge appeared again in England and also in France, Spain, and Germany. From 1144 through the nineteenth century, the blood libel charge appeared, according to historian Walter Lacquer, 150 times.[10] It led to thousands of arrests and deaths throughout Europe. One of the last was in 1881, when a Jesuit organization based in Rome said murder of Gentile children was an integral part of Jewish religion.

Host Desecration

In addition to witnessing the appearance of the blood libel, the medieval period also saw the beginning of an anti-Semitic charge known as *host desecration*. In the thirteenth century, the Eucharist was taking on more and more importance in Christian doctrine and Christian piety. Through the Eucharist,

Christians experienced vicariously the suffering of the cross. As one historian put it, "To eat God was to take into oneself the suffering flesh."[11]

How did newly intense veneration of the Eucharist lead to anti-Semitism? Beginning in the late thirteenth century, Christians began to accuse Jews of stabbing and puncturing the host—the consecrated Eucharistic wafer—and thereby desecrating it. According to these accusations, Jews stabbed and tortured the host just as they had stabbed and tortured Jesus. Host desecration charges appeared throughout France and Germany, galvanizing the murder of thousands of Jews in the fourteenth century. Accounts suggest people believed Jesus actually suffered physically from the Jews' stabbing of the host. Therefore, when authorities arrested Jews accused of host desecration, they would inflict similar torture upon them. Host desecration stories became so popular that they remained common in Europe even after Jews were expelled from most countries. So, even when they were no longer present, Jews could be charged with puncturing and desecrating the body of Jesus.

This strange persistence reminds us that anti-Semitism is not, at its deepest core, about actual Jews. Rather, it gives an answer to a deep psychological need. That need is an explanation for human suffering. All faith traditions need a way of explaining why bad things happen to good people. Anti-Semitism was a way of blaming Jewish wickedness for persistent suffering. The host desecration charge in particular offered a timely, relevant, and potentially comforting message because it showed how Jesus still suffered at the hands of the Jews. Jesus still suffered for the sake of humanity and brought about redemption through that suffering. That he suffered at the hands of the Jews reinforced the truths Christians were taught in church. The desecrated host was an effective way of sustaining the Christian message. "Ironically," as Professor Jeremy Cohen has written, "Jews and the Eucharist together served to make the reality of the cross universal and eternal."[12]

Making Sense of Anti-Semitism

I have taught this history at dozens of churches. And when I do, Christian audiences have the same reaction you might be having: they are distressed, but they wonder what all of this history means today. Consider Holy Week, the period between Palm Sunday and Easter Sunday. What happens during this week? Christians recount and ritually reprise the final week of Jesus's life. The crucifixion story is retold, and communities read the Passion narrative from the Gospel of John—a text that highlights Jewish culpability. The phrase "the Jews" appears repeatedly in the Good Friday readings. John 18:14, for example, discusses the conspiracy to murder Jesus by noting that "Caiaphas [the Jewish high priest] was the one who had advised the Jewish leaders that it was better for one person to die for the people." Further, John 19:14-15 insists that Pilate "said to the Jews, 'Here is your King! They [the Jews] cried out, 'Away with him! Away with him! Crucify him!' " Anyone listening to those words would reasonably conclude that Jews bear significant responsibility for the crucifixion of Jesus.

Holy Week also frequently coincides with the Jewish holiday of Passover. Jesus celebrated Passover. Thus, the overlapping sacred days of Holy Week and Passover could be a time of understanding and shared ritual. But historically, the blood libel charge has usually surfaced during Holy Week (because the blood of the Passover lamb is a central theme of the holiday, and because of the false claim that Jews need the blood of a Christian child to make matzah, the unleavened bread traditionally eaten at the Passover meal).

So, during Holy Week, Christians read a sacred text that depicts Jews murdering Jesus, and their Jewish neighbors are celebrating a holiday in which they discuss the blood of the Passover lamb from Exodus 12. In the fourteenth century, this situation was ripe for violence, and Christians often enacted great violence against Jews during Holy Week. In 1393, for example, hundreds of Jews in Prague were murdered on Easter Sunday. In 1391 in Barcelona, the entire Jewish quarter was destroyed during Holy Week. I read a report recently about a small town in Mexico that, in as late as 2012, held an Easter Sunday parade in which effigies of Jews were carried and then publicly burned.[13]

Twentieth-century literary scholar and anthropologist René Girard can help illumine this Holy Week violence. Girard believed that when things go wrong for a group, as they inevitably will, its members can ask one of two questions: What did they do wrong? Or, who can they blame? When groups ask the second question, they are engaging in the practice of "scapegoating," and in that practice, thought Girard, lay the origins of violence.[14]

Now let's look at the crucifixion of Jesus. From the perspective of the followers of Jesus, his death was not supposed to happen. He was supposed to usher in the messianic era. When he was murdered, how were his followers to respond?

There were many possibilities. One could have said his death was part of the process of redemption, as later theologians did. One could also blame the Romans, as some did as well. But over time, as we have seen, the primary scapegoat became the Jews. Their culpability became central to the narrative—and too often in church history, Christians were incited by Holy Week liturgies to stone, murder, or massacre Jews on Good Friday.

At churches where I speak, I urge Christians to reflect on this history. It is not an easy task. But sometimes faith transforms us when it challenges us. Sacred times can push us to look inward so that we can live with deeper faith and holiness.

I once cited a teaching from the Talmud to show this truth in Judaism. The holiest day of the year for Jews is Yom Kippur, the Day of Atonement. We fast on Yom Kippur and stay in the synagogue in prayer all day. It is meant to be a day of spiritual cleansing. But the Talmud also says that Yom Kippur is the happiest day of the year! How is that possible? Because self-reflection opens up the possibility for change. We can learn. We can grow. And we live differently in the future.

Christian self-reflection on the history of Christian anti-Semitism and violence toward Jews is doubtless painful—but the pain of reflection can lead us ultimately to a more meaningful spiritual life.

Martin Luther and Anti-Semitism in the Protestant Reformation

Much of what we've considered thus far in this chapter is rooted in antiquity (for example, Augustine) or the Middle

Ages (for example, the Crusades and the first host-desecration charges and those charges' resulting violence). So, it might be easy (and for Protestants, comforting) to think that Christian anti-Semitism is located solely or principally in the history of the Catholic Church—but in fact, anti-Semitism also looms large in the very founding of Protestant Christianity. Martin Luther, one of the fathers of the Protestant Reformation, was, in some of his writing, virulent in his denunciations of Judaism and Jews.

Initially, Luther tried to recruit Jews to his church. He believed that many of the Catholic Church's practices were barriers to Jewish conversion—and that when Jews encountered his purified, Protestant Christianity, they would want to convert. When Luther did not succeed in attracting Jewish converts, he lashed out in harsh language, writing, for example, that Jews look for their biblical interpretations in a "pig's anus," and they worship the devil's excrement. As he wrote, "the Devil has emptied ... his stomach again and again, that is a true relic, which the Jews, and those who want to be a Jew, kiss, eat, drink, and worship."[15]

Luther was more violent and outspoken in his proposals for treating Jews than any prominent Christian theologian had ever been. Augustine, for example, never advocated destroying Jewish communities and expelling Jews from countries. But Luther did. In his pamphlet "On the Jews and Their Lies," he urged local governments and communities to take the following actions against Jewish communities:

- Burn all synagogues.
- Destroy Jewish dwellings.

- Confiscate the Jews' holy books.
- Forbid rabbis to teach.
- Forbid Jews to travel.
- Forbid Jews to charge interest on loans to non-Jews and confiscate Jewish property.
- Force Jews to do physical labor.
- Expel the Jews from provinces where they live.[16]

Almost 450 years later, the Nazis consciously followed Luther's suggestions. Hitler even cited Luther as an influence on his thinking about the Jews. Today, Luther's anti-Judaism is a major stain on his reputation. A clergy colleague told me recently that he grew up Lutheran but became a Methodist minister because of Martin Luther's writings about Jews.

Hatred of Jews was one of the few unifying themes of Protestants and Catholics. As Dennis Prager and Joseph Telushkin point out, the Holocaust began in Germany, where the population was almost evenly split between Protestants and Catholics.[17] Both groups had a long tradition of anti-Semitism from which to draw.

Foundations and the Future

Again, we have explored a great deal of history. Does it matter today? For the purposes of this book's brief overview, the key—and troubling—point is that anti-Judaism was one of the foundations of Christianity. The new (the church) had replaced the old (the Jewish people) as the apple of the Father's eye. One famous painting depicts church and synagogue, with the church as a beautiful young woman and the synagogue as a frail, fading, elderly one. The implication is clear. One is vibrant and living. The other is wretched and dying.

This depiction of Judaism permitted and justified Jewish persecution and suffering. If Jews were in league with the devil, they should suffer. If Jews were no longer beloved of God, Christians should persecute them. Therefore, when a series of European countries expelled their Jewish populations, or when the Inquisition exposed Jews to hideous forms of torture, Jews' Christian neighbors largely accepted and even celebrated the destruction of Jews and Jewish communities. The Jews had it coming to them. Their fate was sealed when they murdered the Son of God.

Mike Slaughter

**Author, Speaker, Pastor Emeritus,
Ginghamsburg Church**

As I reflected on this chapter, I couldn't help recalling an experience that I had recently while leading a pastor's retreat in North Carolina. I had arrived at the mountain retreat center early and was sitting by the fireplace in the lodge going over my notes for the two-day event. A couple came in with their son who was there with another group doing a senior thesis film project for graduation from a nearby university.

We introduced ourselves, shared what we did and where we were from. The family was from northern New Jersey. I asked how they met, and they shared that they met each other while growing up in the Bronx. I asked if they went to one of the city public schools, and the mother told me that she went to a private school. For the first time, I noticed some uneasiness in the conversation. "Was it a religious school," I asked. "Yes," she replied with hesitancy. She finally shared that she went to an Orthodox Jewish girls' school and that they were currently practicing "Ortho-Conservative" Jewish faith.

Why the reluctance in sharing? She was afraid of

my response as a Christian pastor. She even shared with me that there was growing anti-Semitism in the area of northern New Jersey where they live.

How far the institutional church has strayed from following the rebel-rabbi Jesus!

6

Is Christianity Still Anti-Semitic?

The Jewish holidays of Rosh Hashanah (the New Year) and Yom Kippur (Day of Atonement) attract more people to worship services than any other days. Whereas most Shabbat services at my synagogue are attended by fifty or a hundred people, these holidays bring at least a thousand people into the synagogue. Thus, my fellow rabbis and I often refer to them as the Jewish Super Bowl. It's our biggest opportunity to speak to our community and inspire them to bring more faith and Jewish meaning into their lives. It is also the time when many people expect a lot from their rabbi. For better or for worse, they may not see me any other time of the year. I want to leave a good impression and feeling. I work on my Rosh Hashanah and Yom Kippur sermons for months, trying to strike the exact right note and speak to the heart as well as the mind.

One year I decided to give a sermon on love. I explored what it means from a Jewish perspective to love God and to love one another. I thought it was a great sermon. Many in my congregation thought differently—at least a dozen people said to me afterward, "Isn't love really a Christian message? We wanted to hear something Jewish. Why did you talk about love?"

It turns out my congregants had absorbed a common but dangerous stereotype: the idea that Christianity is a religion of love and Judaism is a religion of law. They thought that any talk about love and charity was, in some essential way, Christian. Even my own grandfather fell into this trap. I spent a lot of time with him growing up, and when I would do something kind, such as visiting friends of his in a nursing home or shoveling somebody's snow, he would say, "That's very Christian of you."

This is a dangerous stereotype because it draws an absolute distinction between two belief systems—and it implies that one is superior to the other. That is, in most people's minds, love is better than law. Law is about rules and punishment. Love is about forgiveness and kindness. If Christianity is primarily about love, and Judaism is mostly about law, then the former is a kinder, gentler religion than the latter. How did this stereotype develop, and why does it still constitute a dangerous form of anti-Semitism?

Law in Judaism

At the core of Judaism is the Torah. "The Torah" refers to the Five Books of Moses, which were given by God to Moses atop Mount Sinai. But Judaism also has the concept of the oral

Torah. That is, the ongoing commentaries on the Five Books of Moses; the oral Torah includes discussions of and debates about how to live a Jewish life—what to eat when, how much money to give away, how to observe the Sabbath, when to pray, and so on—and Jews understand this oral Torah, not just the Five Books of Moses, to constitute our sacred Scripture. The word *Torah* is a critical one. It means "law," "practice," and "teaching." It does not mean "belief." Thus, at the core of being Jewish is a set of practices, and they begin with laws God gave to Moses at Mount Sinai.

The Torah—the Five Books of Moses—contains 613 laws. Many others were established in the oral Torah. Some of the laws do not apply any longer because they centered around the ancient Jerusalem temple, which no longer stands. And not all Jews follow all the laws—and even in Israel, there is no absolute legal authority to punish a Jew with mandatory jail or fines if he or she does not follow the laws.

Yet, the religion and culture of Judaism cannot be understood without the concept of law. We are members of a religious group with a set of laws. Deed is more important than creed in Judaism. Or, to put it another way, actions are more important than belief. And the primary deeds are laws—often called commandments, or *mitzvot* in Hebrew—that were given by God to Moses and expanded on over time.

Most Important Laws

While, in theory, all the laws are equally important because they come from God, in practice, certain laws become central and often serve to separate Jews from other groups. Two of them are the law regarding circumcision and the kosher dietary traditions. God instructed Abram to circumcise himself and his son Isaac when Isaac was eight days old. Circumcising boys on the eighth day is one of the most commonly observed Jewish laws. The dietary laws are also extensive; they include not eating pork and shellfish or mixing milk and meat.

If there were a moment when Christianity really began to be distinct from Judaism, it is with Paul's understanding that Gentiles did not have to become Jews—in other words, get circumcised and follow dietary laws—in order to become Christian. Indeed, *law* becomes a sort of trope in Paul's writings for those who do not know Jesus, and Paul's denunciation of the law is strong. (See, for example, Romans 5–7.) He said one "isn't made righteous by the works of the Law but rather through the faithfulness of Jesus Christ. We ourselves believed in Christ Jesus so that we could be made righteous by the faithfulness of Christ and not by the works of the Law—because no one will be made righteous by the works of the Law" (Galatians 2:16). For Paul, the Law served as a barrier for people accepting the message of Jesus. It symbolized the flesh while the Spirit spoke to the soul. The Law was directed toward the body while the Spirit lifted up the heart. Following the Law, according to Paul, was not the end goal of God's teaching. Indeed, it seemed that perfectly following the Law was nearly impossible! And Jews had corrupted their relationship with God by focusing intensely on the Law. Their obsession with it distracted people from what was truly important: the death and resurrection of Jesus for the sake of humanity. Therefore, Paul set aside the requirements of Law and accepted Gentiles into the fold if they accepted the truth of the life and death of Jesus.

This change disturbed other Jewish leaders, even some of the initial followers of Jesus, who said the Law should remain in force. Paul is a complex figure to understand because his writings serve multiple purposes. Paul was often debating his fellow Jews. In such conflicts, we expect strong language. Just think of the language we see in political fights today. When Republicans and Democrats hurl insults at each other, they are not meant to define the other side permanently. They can fight one another one minute, and then the next minute have lunch.

Thus, when Paul was criticizing others in the Jesus movement, he was not defining their status for all time. He was simply trying to bring them to his point of view. But when Christianity became the dominant religion of the Western world, Paul's language about the Law become synonymous with Judaism and the Old Testament. Paul's debating points became the defining view of Judaism.

Whether he wanted to or not, Paul effectively severed Christianity from its Jewish roots. The Law was not only wrong—it was dangerous and sinful. Christianity not only replaced Judaism; it proved the backwardness and severity of Judaism itself. Any religion aligned with the Law would entangle its followers in sin, because no one could actually observe every law, all the time. Jesus freed Jews from this trap. But by rejecting his gift, those Jews who clung to the Law perpetuated their sinful ways.

Paul's enduring influence leads many people today to continue to see Judaism as legalistic and harsh. Have you ever heard the phrase "Old Testament justice"? What image comes to mind? It's likely harshness or punishment. After the 2008 financial crisis, many people quoted in newspapers and on television invoked "Old Testament justice" when explaining that they wanted to see bankers imprisoned quickly and severely. A widely shared column by ProPublica, for example, criticized the Securities and Exchanges Commission leader, saying, "Her agency is meekly willing to get token settlements when the situation calls for Old Testament justice."[1] Timothy Geithner, the secretary of the treasury, also mentioned the appetite for "Old Testament vengeance," "Old Testament justice," "Old Testament impulses," "Old Testament populism," "Old Testament cravings," and so forth eighteen times in his book about the financial crisis.[2] The God of the Old Testament is a harsh God. I doubt either Geithner or the author of the ProPublica piece were thinking about Jews when they wrote about "Old Testament justice." But its frequent usage reinforces a view that lets an anti-Semitic stereotype—the idea that Judaism is a religion of law, and that by contrast, Christianity, with its New Testament, is a religion of love and mercy—simmer in the wider culture.

That anti-Semitic stereotype is dangerous—and it is rooted in a misunderstanding of Torah. Consider the verses from the Book of Exodus known as *lex talionis*, which is a Latin phrase meaning "the law of retribution." It reads "If there is further injury, then you will give a life for a life, an eye for an eye, a tooth for a tooth, a hand for a hand, a foot for a foot, a

burn for a burn, a bruise for a bruise, a wound for a wound"
(21:23-25).

These verses may seem strict and harsh. But they have
always been understood by rabbis, scholars, and Jewish
communities as simply conveying the idea of equitable
punishment. That is the basis of all tort law in the Western
world today.

That interpretative tradition matters because when we
read the Bible and make judgments about its adherents, we
need to look at how communities actually enact and inhabit
biblical laws. Would we know how American law works if
we simply looked at the Constitution? No—we have to look
at the amendments and judicial decisions. The same is true in
Judaism.

The rabbinic commentary on Exodus 21 begins by pointing
out that these verses come within a larger biblical section that
deals with economics and business relationships. That context
suggests we should look at these laws within a social and
economic context. Furthermore, the commentators reason,
God's Word has to apply in all circumstances. If an eye for an
eye is meant to be taken literally, they ask, then what do we
do with a blind person who pokes out another person's eyes?
The rhetoric is gruesome, but it makes an important point. The
verses were never meant to be taken literally. They are God's
way of teaching us about justice.

Perhaps some of the venom hurled at Jews on the basis of
these verses has a psychological dimension. Christianity emerged
out of Judaism. Judaism is like the father, and Christianity is
like the son. The Old Testament God, therefore, is portrayed

as a bad father: difficult to please, stubborn, domineering. He is materialistic, and he lacks spirituality. This father's love has to be earned. It is not given by grace. This view leads to the conclusion that Judaism is the stubborn father clinging to the past, while Christianity is the young, vibrant son looking to the future. The father dwells on law while the son seeks only love.

When Is the Law/Love Dichotomy Anti-Semitic?

Does any discussion of the different ways Christianity and Judaism think about law and love always constitute anti-Semitism? No. Law is an integral part of Judaism, and it is fair and useful to point out where Judaism and Christianity differ. What is anti-Semitic, however, is suggesting that Jewish commitment to law is at odds with the ethic of love. To caricature Judaism as a faith whose adherents will always and blindly follow the Law, even if doing so leads to human suffering, is anti-Semitic. To connect a desire for revenge and extreme punishment with the Old Testament God is anti-Semitic. To see law as the sole focus of Judaism, to ignore the way Jews have read the Bible and actually lived in history, and to imagine that a reverence for law rules out a reverence for love is anti-Semitic.

As we know from looking at Paul, the stereotype of Judaism as legalistic and vengeful dates to the first decades of the church. The Gospel writers regularly contrast the mercy of Jesus with the narrowness of the scribes. We need to point out a critical historical truth. The Old Testament remained a part of Christianity, and Jesus did not call the Old Testament vengeful and legalistic. Rather, he cited it continuously—indeed, he was drawing on Deuteronomy and Leviticus when he said that the greatest commandments, the most important laws, are "Love the LORD your God with all your heart, all your being, and all your strength" and "Love your neighbor as yourself" (Deuteronomy 6:5; Leviticus 19:18). Thus, the stereotype of the Old Testament as legalistic and unloving did not have to become a prominent part of Christianity. And among many Christians today, it is not. Indeed, many Christians embrace and study the Old Testament, sometimes even reading the Old Testament through the lens of traditional Jewish interpretation. Nonetheless, stereotypes of Christianity as loving and Judaism as legalistic persist.

I've already noted that people today often use the phrase "Old Testament justice" as a shorthand for vengeful, disproportionate applications of law. We should also look out for the word *Talmudic*. It is occasionally used in the same way. A person is being "Talmudic" in following or sticking to the Law. Or "Talmudic logic" is used to suggest someone is trying to confuse or deceive someone else with complex ideas and far-fetched logic. Using the word *Talmudic* in this way connects a sacred Jewish text to deception and manipulation. The more we notice words being put to prejudicial use, the more we combat anti-Semitic speech.[3]

Jesus Was Jewish

Another anti-Semitic move that persists in Christianity today is the erasure of Jesus's Jewishness. When I tell people about an earlier book I wrote on the Jewishness of Jesus, they often say, "So what? Everyone knows Jesus was Jewish." But that's only half true.

Many Christians (and Jews) believe Jesus *used to be* Jewish: he was born Jewish but his Jewishness was replaced by Christianity when he was baptized by John the Baptist. Bill O'Reilly, for example, who wrote the #1 *New York Times* best seller *Killing Jesus*, echoes this view and lambasts those who disagree with him. During an episode of his television show, O'Reilly said that scholars' note "that Christianity didn't exist in Jesus' lifetime and he never proposed a new religion" have run "off the rails" and give "false" accounts of history.[4] The argument of O'Reilly and others who believe Jesus left Judaism and began a new religion has dangerous consequences. Here's why: if Jesus is God, the implication of O'Reilly's view is that God rejected Judaism and replaced it with a new faith. Seeing Jesus as leaving Judaism is another form of supersessionism. And this erasure of Jesus's Jewishness gives some credence to those who believe that the Jews hated Jesus because he left their religion.

O'Reilly is not the first person to minimize Jesus's Judaism. Throughout history, many Christians have erased Jesus's Judaism. Consider, for example, medieval, Renaissance, and modern art. In the hundreds of thousands of depictions of Jesus, we see very few signs of his Jewish identity. As Dr. Bernard Starr (one of the scholars with whom O'Reilly takes issue) puts it in describing Renaissance art, "Jesus is typically portrayed as northern European in appearance, embedded in anachronistic later-day palatial Christian settings surrounded by Christian artifacts—all totally alien to his ethnicity, religion and identity as a practicing Jew who resided in a rural Galilean village." A result of this portrayal, Dr. Starr explains, is that "wherever the Renaissance Christian populace turned—in churches, public spaces and homes—they would only see images of a totally Christian Jesus."[5]

That imagery was especially important in shaping people's perceptions because literacy was not widespread until the nineteenth century. Perhaps if elements of Jesus's Jewishness had been portrayed in Christian art, we would have seen less anti-Semitism. As we saw in chapter 5, medieval art conflated Jews and the devil. Jews were portrayed with horns and tails and malicious intent. Artists would have been less likely to use such portrayals if Jesus were depicted as a Jew as well.

A New Bridge

Jesus lived and died as a Jew. He never rejected Judaism. He lived Judaism and taught Judaism—and a new application of Jesus's teachings emerged after his death. Both those who see Jesus as a great human teacher and those who accept him as God incarnate can appreciate the religious life he lived as described in the Gospels. Recovering and deepening our understanding of this Jewish Jesus—seeing Jesus as a bridge between Judaism and Christianity—is part of helping foster connection instead of distrust between Jews and Christians.

Some disagree with this view. One rabbinic colleague of mine hosts several interfaith scholarly conferences. He invites Jewish and Christian scholars to address various issues and seek to find common ground. He refuses, however, to invite any scholar who was previously Christian and converted to Judaism, or anyone born Jewish who converted to Christianity. He believes acknowledging the legitimacy of such people undermines fundamental truths at the heart of each religion. I understand my colleague's view, but, honestly, I think it lacks humility. Humility demands that each of us recognize that we are equipped only with the capacity to understand God from our point of view. It further demands that we recognize that we do not know everything and that we do not have a monopoly on the path to God.

Humility does not mean we are meek or half-hearted in our faith. In my experience, those who have been most passionately interested in deepening their understanding of the Jewishness of Jesus are strong in their Christian and Jewish faiths—indeed, interfaith appreciation often comes from deeply committed believers and practitioners because it is exactly when we are serious about our faith that we realize how important faith is to others as well. It is when we recognize the way faith shapes our own lives that we better appreciate the way it enriches the lives of others.

Faith is not zero-sum. The strength of my convictions do not take away from someone else's different convictions. Rather, each person's beliefs can grow stronger as we learn from one another. Think about a set of candles. One light does not take away from the other. Rather, each candle can light another. And when that happens, more light is created.

A recent experience illustrated this truth for me. It came shortly after a Chicago synagogue was vandalized. Tension filled the community. The recent upsurge in anti-Semitism was on everyone's mind. I was invited to the North Park Christian Seminary in Chicago to offer a blessing at a ceremony where they would dedicate a Torah scroll. I was a little puzzled by the request. Torah scrolls are expensive and difficult to attain, and they are typically only used in synagogue. Why would a Christian seminary want one? I then learned more about it.

The Torah scroll had been donated by a man named Ken Larson. In the 1960s he started a store in Minneapolis called Slumberland. It sold home furniture. He opened more stores. Then he branched into franchising. Now Slumberland operates 126 stores.

Ken was always active in his church. When he had retired six years before, he and his wife, Barbara, took their extended family on a trip to Israel, where they viewed some ancient Torah scrolls. Their guide told them about the way the scroll was written—by hand, letter by letter. It took a scribe an entire year to write one scroll. Ken and Barbara had never seen one before. And in the presence of their first Torah school, they had never felt closer to God's Word.

When they got back to Minnesota, Ken and Barbara approached their local seminary in Minneapolis. Ken, who was on the seminary board, asked if the seminary had a Torah scroll. When the president said no, Ken and Barbara donated one. They saw the excitement it brought the faculty and students. They saw the way it brought students to life. Then they asked themselves, "Is God calling us to a new ministry?"

The Larsons teamed up with a scholar named Scott Carroll. With Dr. Carroll's help, they purchased scrolls from collectors around the world and donated each scroll to a different seminary. So far, they have given away thirty-one scrolls! Their only stipulation is that the scroll cannot be stuck in a basement or a closet. It must be used and celebrated.

When I heard his story, I realized I could not turn down the request to participate. Millions of Jews had been murdered for their love of and commitment to Torah. Hundreds of Torah scrolls had been burned in Nazi Germany. And now a Christian couple was dedicated to bringing Torah scrolls to seminaries creating the next generation of Christian leaders.

At the beginning of the dedication ceremony, we carried the scroll into the school's chapel. One of the students read from it. Then I offered a blessing. I had done a little research and learned that this particular Torah scroll came from a town in Poland in the late eighteenth century, and in my blessing, I spoke about the creation of that particular scroll. The scribe who wrote it probably lived in a tiny ramshackle house, and he likely worked on it for at least a year. He would never have imagined that the words he was writing would be studied three hundred years later—in Chicago, Illinois—by Christian seminary students.

It was another reminder of what we all know. God works—and builds bridges—in mysterious ways.

Still, despite the bridges we have crossed, large chasms remain. One of the areas where the stereotype of the deceitful Jew remains is in discourse about money. To consider that, we turn to the next chapter.

Justin Coleman

Senior Pastor, University United Methodist Church

Is Christianity at its core, anti-Semitic? The short answer is no. Are Christians anti-Semitic anyway? Unfortunately, that answer is sometimes yes. In this chapter, Rabbi Evan Moffic does a good job at addressing that "sometimes yes."

Christianity has its roots in Judaism. So how does anti-Semitism sometimes emerge from a religion that is so grounded in Judaism?

Because Christians forget.

I was once having lunch with a parishioner at a barbecue restaurant. We were discussing the book of Acts as he was having pork ribs. (Yes, this happens when you are a pastor.) I said, "You know that you wouldn't be able to eat those ribs were it not for Acts 15, right?" He, of course, wanted to know what I meant. I pointed out that this was the chapter when Paul and other Jewish leaders decided to remove certain dietary and other requirements for Gentiles as they became part of this very Jewish religious movement that would become known as Christianity. My friend said that he'd simply forgotten that all the people in that chapter of Acts were Jewish. This is a simple oversight that can lead to the larger ramifications that Rabbi Moffic lifts up in this chapter. The danger is a Gentile-washing of Christianity's religious history.

Rabbi Moffic has done an excellent job in highlighting portions of poor interpretation from some Christians that still lead to aggression from some who would call themselves Christian. I hope that those who read these pages will be inspired to think about and interpret Scripture in ways that are consonant with what we know of Jesus through our reading of Scripture with growing understanding of Jewish life, interpretation, and tradition.

7

"He Jewed Me Down"

Money and Anti-Semitism

Like most Americans, by the last weeks of the 2016 election season, I was ready for the campaign to end. Campaign season had been long and messy. It was also filled with anger. By Halloween, I thought I had seen everything. But then a commercial made me realize I had not. This commercial showed me just how powerful the resurgence of anti-Semitism had become.

The commercial begins with ominous music. Then it introduces us to the "global power structure" who deceive ordinary Americans. They enrich themselves and leave everyone else worse off. Four people—people who are supposedly pulling the levers behind this power structure—are featured in the commercial. One of them is Hillary Clinton. That is not surprising. She was one of the candidates.

The other three, however, seemingly had no relationship

to one another. One (Janet Yellen) worked for the government. Another (George Soros) was a retired hedge fund manager and major political donor. The third (Lloyd Blankfein) worked for an investment bank. The only thing they had in common was that they worked in finance and were Jewish. They had now become the faces for a narrative about the vast global conspiracy designed to rob ordinary Americans of their hard-earned wealth. The language used to describe them and this conspiracy echoed charges that had been hurled against Jews for centuries: Jews are secretive, manipulative, and do not care about national borders. They care only for money and enriching themselves.

One nonpartisan analysis of the commercial examined the subtle ways the ad reinforced this anti-Semitism: "The Jews come up to punctuate specific key phrases: Soros, 'those who control the levers of power in Washington'; Yellen, 'global special interests'; Blankfein, 'put money into the pockets of a handful of large corporations.' "[1] In other words, as the commercial discusses people who control the economy for their own benefit, visual images of these famous Jews come up. I am sure many people who saw the commercial did not immediately think of Jews. But many did, as evidenced by the reactions from both sides of the political aisle. The implied message was that the economy is rigged by selfish globalist Jews.

That stereotype, in various guises, is a staple of twenty-first-century discourse. During the 2008 financial crisis, for example, a representative comment on a prominent website said "Just another Jew money changer thief. It's been happening for 3,000 years. Trust a Jew and this is what will happen. History has proven it over and over. Jews have only one god—money."[2] During that same crisis, financier Bernard Madoff was accused of creating a Ponzi scheme that robbed his clients of $65 billion. His Jewishness was highlighted in many of the articles about him. In the *New York Times*, for example, a profile of Madoff used the word *Jewish* three times in its first nine short paragraphs. In contrast, when a similar story about a Ponzi scheme run by Allen Stanford was exposed, his religion was not mentioned at all.[3] A pattern emerged in the coverage of Madoff: a prominent news site such as the *Huffington Post* or a newspaper like the *Palm Beach Post* would write a story about Madoff, and the story would include extensive discussion of his religious background. Then a flurry of anti-Semitic comments would flow in.

In surveying the news coverage, the Anti-Defamation League concluded that the stories themselves were not anti-Semitic. But they did encourage readers to focus on Madoff's religion as if it had some connection with his crime. By doing so, they invited anti-Semitic views. This was just the latest and most prominent example of the enduring stereotype of the greedy, unscrupulous Jew.[4]

This chapter will unpack how this stereotype developed and why it is likely to persist. The world is becoming more complex and interconnected. Money pervades our everyday lives—we seek it, we rely on it, and we struggle with it. As a response to our confusion and frustration about money, we often look for a scapegoat—someone to blame for the financial complexities of the world, or someone to blame for our own financial situation. Jews have been that scapegoat for centuries.

The Beginning

Greedy Jews were a scapegoat in one of the Gospels' most notable stories: Jesus's overturning the tables of the money changers in the Jerusalem temple.

The story goes like this: Jesus charged that the money changers had corrupted God's house and hurt the poor widows whose money they took. Jesus was restoring the Temple and cleansing it from the corrupt priests who benefited from those greedy money changers. This story appears in all four Gospels, indicating its importance.

The problem with the story is not the story itself—it is how people have sometimes interpreted the Gospels' accounts of Jesus overturning those tables. First, we have to understand why the money changers existed in the first place. They were cogs in a system. They served an important function in that they made it possible for people from all over the ancient Near East who could not physically bring an animal sacrifice with them to obtain one at the temple. Many interpret the money changers as openly violating sacred norms by overcharging the poor and ignorant while their overseers—the priests—turned a blind eye and likely profited from their corruption. And yet, Jesus was not against the Temple. He was not opposed to money changing. He was opposed to the corruption that harmed the poor and the ignorant. He was calling out the priests who profited from it.

Jesus's anger at them was shared by many Jewish leaders. Indeed, like Jesus, one of the most prominent rabbis of the era—Shimon ben Gamaliel (son of Gamaliel, the apostle Paul's personal spiritual teacher)—publicly lambasted the price gouging happening at the Temple.

Over time, however, the money changers began, in the public imagination, to symbolize Jews in general. Anti-Semites were only too happy to put biblical language to work in depicting Jews as greedy and corrupt, as in the previously quoted website comment during the 2008 financial crisis: "Just another Jew money changer thief. It's been happening for 3,000 years."[5]

For the Love of Money

Why have anti-Semites portrayed Jews as greedy and deceptive? In part because they were outsiders in Christian societies where Jews often performed essential roles deemed off-limits for Christians. During the medieval period, the most important of these was moneylending. The church prohibited Christians from lending money at interest because doing so was considered "unnatural" because money cannot beget money. Yet, credit is essential for an economy to grow, and medieval communities needed a way to lend money if they wanted to build wealth. Therefore, many leaders, including local bishops, invited Jews to their towns to serve as moneylenders. This profession was especially attractive to Jews because they could not own land or belong to professional guilds. Moneylending was one of the few ways for Jews to earn a living.[6]

But if moneylending is forbidden in the Old Testament, how could Jews practice it? Remember how we noted that Jews always read the Bible with commentary? Well, the commentary suggests that lending money with interest is not prohibited. Rather, lending money at prohibitively high rates constitutes usury. So long as interest rates are reasonable, lending money is permitted.

Furthermore, the commentators noted that the laws in the Torah addressed a situation when Jews were living in their own independent nation, not in Christian states in Europe. Jews faced extra taxes in Europe and could not enter numerous professions. Therefore, lending money was a means of survival. And since many local bishops offered Jews protection if they moved to their towns and lent money, it promised a degree of safety as well. In Jewish tradition, a means of saving lives trumps almost every commandment. Therefore, moneylending became a viable occupation. While the vast majority of Jews were shopkeepers or farmers or had other typical occupations in the Middle Ages, a small number became moneylenders.

While moneylending helped save lives and support the Jewish community, it came with a dark side. When economies experienced downturns, Jews were often blamed.

Local leaders also took advantage of the theologically based prejudice against Jews to channel public anger during crises. When the Black Plague spread throughout Europe in the fourteenth century, for example, Jews were blamed for the deaths in their communities, and they were targeted by mobs, who stole from them, sometimes forced them to be baptized, and even murdered them. What does this have to do with economics and stereotypes of rich, greedy Jews? An account written in 1349 spells out the connection:

> On Saturday—that was St. Valentine's Day—they burnt the Jews on a wooden platform in their cemetery. There were about two thousand people of them. Those who wanted to baptize themselves were spared. Many small children were taken out of the fire and baptized against the will of their fathers and mothers. And everything that was owed to the Jews was cancelled, and the Jews had to surrender all pledges and notes that they had taken for debt. The council, however, took the cash that the Jews possessed and divided it among the workingmen proportionately. The money was indeed the thing that killed the Jews. If they had been poor and if the feudal lords had not been in debt to them, they would not have been burned.[7]

Along with many scholars, I still struggle to understand why Jews have so frequently been castigated as greedy, cheap, and willing to do anything for money. Jews were not noticeably wealthier than other groups. Indeed, in medieval Europe, most Jews—like most Christians—lived with modest financial means or even in outright poverty. Their lives were, as Thomas Hobbes famously put it, "nasty, brutish and short."[8]

One potential explanation is projection—the idea that

anti-Semites accuse Jews of crimes of which the accusers are guilty. They may see Jews as embodying traits they dislike in themselves. A concrete example of projection happened during the trial of Alfred Dreyfus.

Middlemen Minority

Another psychological dimension behind economic anti-Semitism comes from Jews frequently occupying the role of what Professor Thomas Sowell calls a "middleman minority."[9] The middleman minorities fuel the relationship between the producers and the consumers. They are the retailers selling goods produced somewhere else to local consumers. They are the bankers lending money to both producers and consumers, and thereby facilitating economic exchange between the two groups.

Middleman minorities do not only serve this intermediary economic role. They also serve as an intermediary between different social groups, and frequently between different socioeconomic classes within a country. In Catholic Poland, for example, Jews were the intermediaries between the small group of wealthy landowners and the large group of peasants who paid taxes to these landowners.

This economic role had some advantages. It allowed Jews (and other minorities, like the Lebanese in Africa or the Chinese in Indonesia) to maintain their identities. Being different from the larger culture—being a minority—made the middlemen more effective in their role because the different classes or groups were able to relate more effectively through a third party.

Serving as an intermediary, however, also presents acute dangers. First, when prices are high or an economy is in decline, the middlemen are often blamed. They are simply closer and more visible to the people who are suffering. Secondly, because the middleman minority are, by definition, a minority, they are more susceptible to anger from the masses. They provide a unifying target.

A third and more subtle danger lurks in the perception that middlemen are earning a profit without producing anything of value. That perception can quickly translate into violence. As Sowell points out:

> Those who earned their livings without visible toil, with clean hands, and by simply selling things that others had produced at higher prices than the producers had charged, were ready targets of resentments, especially when these non-producers enjoyed a higher standard of living than those who worked in factories or on farms. It did not have to be a dramatically higher standard of living. Those nearby on the socioeconomic scale are often more hotly resented than distant rich people.[10]

In other words, resentment did not come because Jews were much richer than the larger population. It came because of the role they played and their proximity to the consumer.

Evolving Economy

As we noted, other groups occupied the middleman minority role, including the Lebanese in West Africa, the

Chinese in parts of the Near East, and the Armenians in the Ottoman Empire. The Jewish story is unique, however, because Jews lacked a homeland for almost two thousand years. They lived as a minority everywhere they resided. Their identity as a people in the eyes of others was linked to their economic role. They were the intermediary between rich and poor, between the producer and the consumer. This role as economic middlemen sheds light on the persistence of anti-Semitism because of the evolution of the economy.

The modern economy is one in which consumers have grown increasingly distant from the producer. In other words, trade and capitalism have created more distance between the beneficiaries and producers of goods. They have enhanced the role of the middleman. An early example of the way this economic evolution fostered anti-Semitism is in Shakespeare's play *The Merchant of Venice*. It was written between 1596 and 1599, and economist Eric Gans points out that it captures the shift in Europe from feudalism to capitalism, from a society based on hierarchical rituals to one based on market forces. Status relationships are replaced by contractual ones. This shift disorientated many, including those who benefited from it.[11]

At the center of the shift in Shakespeare's play is Shylock, a Jewish moneylender. Shylock is the foil for Antonio, a Christian merchant. Antonio's friend takes out a loan from Shylock, which Antonio guarantees. But Antonio has angered Shylock in the past because of his anti-Semitism. Still, Shylock agrees to the loan on the condition that he may take a "pound of flesh" from Antonio if he fails to repay it.

As the story is developing, we learn that Shylock's daughter Jessica has eloped, converted to Christianity, and taken a significant portion of Shylock's money, even as she claims to despise his greed. In this scenario, we have, as anthropologist Melanie Long points out, a clear portrayal of anti-Semitism. "Shylock," she wrote, "lives up to popular perceptions of both usurers and Jews in the early modern period: he treasures wealth as much as, if not more than his own daughter and hounds for a Christian's pound of flesh in an echo of the 'blood libel' that fueled early persecution of Jews."[12]

The rest of the play confirms this perception. When Antonio cannot pay back his loan on time, Shylock insists on taking his pound of flesh. When Antonio's friend offers to pay back twice the amount of the loan, Shylock refuses. He is determined to take his pound of Christian flesh. Ultimately, however, the Jewish stereotype of legalism is turned against Shylock.

Another character, Portia, says Shylock is only permitted to take flesh and not blood, and if any blood spills from Antonio, he violates the terms of the agreement and thereby forfeits his reward and his land. Furthermore, he is only permitted a pound of flesh, no more and no less. When Shylock then agrees to accept the money from Antonio's friend, he is told he cannot take it because he is an alien who attempted to take the life of a citizen, and he must convert to Christianity or lose his entire estate. The only choice he has that permits him to live is to convert and promise his entire estate to his daughter Jessica and her husband, Lorenzo. Shylock is utterly defeated and humiliated, economically and religiously. His greed and lack of patriotism ensure his demise.

This play leaves the impression that Jews are merciless, greedy, vengeful, and desirous of Christian blood, and it captures many elements of traditional and modern anti-Semitism: not just the desire for vengeance and an overarching greed, but also stubbornness, a lack of commitment to the state, and a sense of superiority. The fact that Shylock was a moneylender helped seal this image of the Jew and the associated stereotypes for centuries. On the night of November 9-10, 1938, in a precursor to the Holocaust, hundreds of synagogues were destroyed across Germany and dozens of Jews were murdered—the event quickly became known as *Kristallnacht* ("Night of Crystal," referring to all the glass that was broken as synagogue after synagogue was destroyed). Shortly after Kristallnacht, *The Merchant of Venice* began to play frequently over German radio.

With this history in mind, I was both taken aback and intrigued to receive in 2015 an invitation to serve on a panel following a production of *The Merchant of Venice* at a Jewish community center in Skokie, Illinois. Skokie is a city near Chicago with a disproportionately large number of Holocaust survivors. A neo-Nazi march in the 1970s in Skokie sparked massive protests and lawsuits. Showing *The Merchant of Venice* in Skokie seemed like an invitation for anger and hurt.

It ended up being an extraordinary experience. As a priest on the panel, Father Michael Sparough taught me and the audience about how damaging and influential the play had been. Father Sparough, a former Shakespearean actor, explored the religious and historical contexts to help us understand economic anti-Semitism even further.

First, Father Sparough talked about how Shylock had been portrayed in earlier renditions of the play. Up until the late twentieth century, he said, Shylock was almost always portrayed as the devil incarnate. His house is described as "hell." He is referred to as the devil who quotes Scripture. Perhaps the most famous reference comes from the character Solanio, who sees Shylock approaching and says, "Let me say Amen betimes, least the divell cross my praier, for here he comes in the likenes of a Jew." As we learned in chapter 6, "the devil in the likeness of a Jew" is a way we can describe many medieval artistic portrayals of the devil. Here Shakespeare connects that representation to Jews' economic role. The devil is greedy. The devil is materialistic. And so are Jews.

Shakespeare goes even further in contrasting the Jews' greed and desire for vengeance with Christian mercy and kindness. When the character Bassanio invites Shylock to his home for dinner, Shylock declines, saying he will do business with him but not eat, drink, or pray with him. Shylock's refusal to accept double the amount of his original loan as a repayment from Antonio's friend highlights the contrast between Christian generosity and support for a friend with the Jewish Shylock's desire for Christian flesh. The message is both familiar in its history and shocking in its grotesqueness.

Father Sparough also helped me understand that this

form of anti-Semitism reflects changes in Christian culture. The seventeenth century was the time when the Calvinist movement grew. Calvinism was an outgrowth of the Protestant Reformation, and its followers saw worldly success as a sign of divine favor. This emphasis on the divinity of wealth clashed with Catholic doctrine and renewed the stereotype of Jews as deceptive and greedy. The sixteenth century saw a wave of plays, including *The Merchant of Venice* and *The Jew of Malta* by Christopher Marlowe, in which Jews were depicted as devilish exemplars of the evils of capitalism. Other important stories from the time—like the German legend of Faust—associated Jews with greed and materialism.

The timing is critical. The Thirty Years' War brought about a freer religious environment in Europe, where different Protestant groups and Catholics slowly began to live together. The market economy was leading to growing wealth that challenged the prevailing feudal system. Europe was changing, but the villain remained the same. Jews still occupied the role of devil. But their devilry came from economic manipulation. That greed complemented the religious heresy for which they had long been guilty. Anti-Semitism did not diminish as Europe moved from the medieval to the modern period. Rather, it mutated.

One of the reasons it could successfully do so is that Jews had been expelled from much of western Europe during the fourteenth and fifteenth centuries. By the seventeenth and eighteenth centuries, Jews were readmitted, largely for economic reasons: Jews had established themselves in the moneylending field. This expertise proved useful in the changing economic world. But that readmittance—along with the cycles of boom and bust that came with economic change—led to new expressions of anti-Semitism.

This readmittance and the accompanying economic anti-Semitism exemplify another psychological dimension of bigotry. It is what psychologists call the "independence-dependence conflict." We often hate those on whom we depend because they symbolize our lack of independence—that's why an elderly parent might lash out at the adult child she depends on.

That conflict happened on a broader scale in Europe in the relationship between Christians and Jews. First, the economic development of Europe depended on moneylending. Many European nobles depended on "court Jews" who would loan them money for conquests and land purchases. In turn, those peasants who relied on local nobles for their livelihood indirectly depended upon Jews.

This relationship of economic dependence lay atop an earlier and deeper dependence: The roots of Christianity lay in Judaism, and in a fundamental way, Christianity depended on Judaism. Several early Christian thinkers tried to sever those roots out of a fear that they undermined the divinity of Jesus. That is, the existence of Judaism itself suggested the message of Jesus was not fully accepted by his fellow Jews. Yet, early Christian theologians developed the idea that Jews suffer as punishment for their sins and serve as evidence for the waywardness of those who do not accept Jesus. A similar logic applied in economic terms. The developing economies of Europe depended on lending and markets. They were necessary evils. Those who created them survived but suffered.

We see this exact scenario in *The Merchant of Venice*. Several of the main characters depend on Shylock. Antonio depends on him for loans so that he can run his shipping business. The beginning of the play makes clear they have done business together many times before, despite Antonio's insults toward Shylock. Shylock's daughter depends on him for financial support. At the end of the play, the duke depends on Shylock for money for his duchy. Even though Shylock is the villain of the play, he is also the central axis on which it all turns. Without his existence, the happy ending would not come about. A broader implication follows this truth. Christianity is not possible without Jews. Modern Europe is not possible without Jews. Like Shylock, Jews are essential, and they are hated.

Conclusion

I mentioned earlier the quip that the entire world Jewish population would be considered a small statistical error in the Chinese census. The author who made that quip, Milton Himmelfarb, went on to say that "each of us Jews knows how thoroughly ordinary he is; yet taken together, we seem caught up in things great and inexplicable. It is almost as if we were not acting but were being acted through."[13] The story of Jews in the modern world bears out Himmelfarb's observation. Its economic, political, and social tensions were acted out through a nation's treatment of its Jews. Sadly, the stereotype of the greedy Jew remains potent and influential. It may become more so as the divide between rich and poor continues to grow and those left behind look for people to blame. Indeed, that has been the trend in the modern world, which I date to the onset of the French Revolution in 1789. We turn now to how the modern world unfolded and to the additional expressions of anti-Semitism that emerged.

Katharine Jefferts Schori

Former Presiding Bishop of the Episcopal Church

Some fifteen years ago I was standing in a rural town's cemetery waiting to bury a deeply faithful, retired priest. Another Christian pastor and friend of that priest stood with me waiting for the hearse, chatting about local events. I was shocked to hear him say that a local businessman had "jewed him down." I couldn't quite believe my ears, but I gathered my wits and told him I was deeply offended, that I considered Jews our elder siblings in faith and that I hoped he would revise his language and thinking. It was a powerful example of how anti-Semitism has worked its way into our daily lives.

In 1920s Germany, Jews were prospering while Germans were struggling. This led to some Germans becoming envious of their Jewish neighbors. An excellent NPR program explored the move from envy to *schadenfreude* (joy at another's misfortune) in the face of competition. Shankar Vedantam discussed research about this pattern using college sports as an example and then went on to explore responses encouraged by the

Nazi regime to the perceived prosperity of Jews and the Jewish community.*

Envy and fear drive a great deal of unexamined reaction, and assigning the label of *other* is a frequent response. Nazi Germany painted the Jews as "the others." The core of the Christian gospel is about loving God with one's whole being and loving one's neighbor as oneself. It is also the heart of Judaism. There is no ultimate *other* in our religious tradition; all are beloved children of God, and all deserve the care, concern, and compassion of every human being. The Christian Gospels are filled with teaching about loving the despised, the foreigner, those who abuse, and even the occupying Romans.

The *other* will be with us as long as we cannot see a reflection of the divine—when we do, we discover blessing, and the One who blesses all that is. Seek life and wholeness and blessing, and you will find *haShem*, who gives life and light and learning and love to all creation.

* Shankar Vedantam, host, *Hidden Brain*, "Feeding the Green-Eyed Monster: What Happens When Envy Turns Ugly," National Public Radio, February 26, 2018, www.npr.org/templates/transcript/transcript.php?storyId=586674547.

8

"A Messianic Promise and a Demonic Reality"

Anti-Semitism in the Modern World

A nineteenth-century Jewish folktale tells of a rabbi sitting behind his desk, studying and stroking his beard. A visitor arrives and begins telling the rabbi about all the wonderful things happening in the world. A new factory has been built in his town. One of his children has started studying at a university in Germany. Another child has set off to settle in America.

The rabbi smiles and turns to the man and says, "That is wonderful, my friend, wonderful. Things are good. Thank God," he says. "But tell me: if things are so good, why are they so bad?"

The rabbi's comments give us a window into anti-Semitism in the modern period, which begins in the seventeenth and eighteenth centuries and continues into the twentieth. Prior to the Holocaust, life had improved for many Jews. They had left the ghettos and settled in better neighborhoods with stable jobs. They entered universities previously closed to them. They became citizens of the states where they had once been barely tolerated aliens. The era promised intellectual and political freedom. The French Revolution proclaimed equality, brotherhood, and liberty, and enlightened thinkers such as Voltaire critiqued the religious prejudices that had been part of European life for centuries.

And for many, this promise was realized. My great-grandparents would not have been able to leave Poland and Austria had not thinkers such as John Locke and Thomas Jefferson articulated the ideas that led to the American Constitution. The intellectual and political movements for reason and freedom—known respectively as the Enlightenment and the emancipation—changed Europe and the religious groups residing there.

But there was also an underbelly. Freedom in theory did not mean equality in practice. Deep-seated hatreds did not disappear with a new form of government. And as more Jews interacted with Christians, more justifications for anti-Semitism arose. In the nineteenth century, the Christian threads that had held anti-Semitism together for so many centuries remained, but they were stitched into new forms of political and social scapegoating, and sequined with faux science. This scapegoating gave energy to the most destructive expressions of anti-Semitism in history: the Holocaust. Here's how it happened.

From the Renaissance to Modernity

By the end of the medieval period, Jews had been exiled from much of western Europe. This expulsion led to a large-scale migration of Jews to central and eastern Europe. By the seventeenth century, millions of Jews lived in Poland, Russia, the Ukraine, and the Baltic countries. These areas were largely Catholic and Eastern Orthodox, and many of the medieval Christian stereotypes persisted. Yet, local rulers and landowners often found having Jews in their communities to be economically beneficial because Jews could serve as moneylenders, which produced economic growth; in addition, Jews often served as land managers and rent collectors for elite landowners. Each of these roles reinforced that association between Jews and money, as we saw in chapter 7. As in western Europe, Jews were forbidden to enter trade and artistic guilds unless they converted to the majority religion, which in this case was Orthodox Christianity.

In the eighteenth century, Poland became a part of Russia, which was the dominant power in the region. The Russian government designated a large area, including Poland and other conquered areas with large Jewish populations, as the "Pale of Settlement." Jews were required to live within the settlement and could not migrate into interior Russia. While the Russian Orthodox Church did not develop deep anti-Jewish theological views in the same way as did the Catholic Church, it professed strong anti-Jewish sentiment, and the close ties between the church and the tsarist regime led to targeted Jewish persecution. Russian ruler Peter the

Great said, "I prefer to see in our midst nations professing Mohammedanism and paganism rather than Jews. They are rogues and cheats. It is my endeavor to eradicate evil, not to multiply it."[1]

For the small percentage of Jews remaining in western Europe during the Renaissance, little improved. In 1555, Pope Paul IV issued a papal bull revoking Jewish rights to live in certain neighborhoods, mandating that Jews listen to a Catholic sermon on the Jewish Sabbath, and restricting Jewish entry into the medical profession. That same year, the pope also established a Jewish ghetto in Rome, which was a walled-in area in one of the most flood-prone parts of Rome where the city's two thousand Jews had to live. When leaving the ghetto area for work, Jewish men had to wear a yellow star on their clothing and women a yellow veil. The ghetto was locked from the outside during major Christian holidays, like Christmas and Easter, so Jews could not leave.

The Roman ghetto was the second major ghetto in Europe (the first, the Venetian ghetto, had been established in 1516). Over the next three hundred years, ghettos were built in many European cities. They differed in their restrictions—some were locked from the outside every evening—but they generally housed a large majority of a community's Jewish population in impoverished and unsanitary conditions. A few Jews—scholars estimate less than 1 percent—became financially successful by serving as financiers to local rulers. These were known as court Jews. Court Jews helped local rulers fight wars, but they often became the victim of populist anger when wars failed or when economies declined.

The Persistence of Christian Anti-Semitism in the Modern Era

The emergence of the modern nation-state in the seventeenth and eighteenth centuries undermined the power of the church in western and central Europe. But the emerging nation-states often integrated anti-Semitism into their political philosophies and programs as well. And one persistent church doctrine is critical in understanding the destructiveness of anti-Semitism in the modern era. That is the doctrine developed during the Spanish Inquisition called *limpieza de sangre*, "purity of blood." According to this doctrine, even Jews who had converted to Christianity, as many would do, were under suspicion of remaining Jewish and were barred from holding public office in Spain. Some historians suggest the Inquisition was more interested in this group—known as *conversos*—than they were in Jews who refused to convert to Christianity.

This purity-of-blood doctrine introduced a racial element into what had once been only a religious hatred. A Jew was Jewish by race, and that racial identity was increasingly understood to be immutable.

The concept of Judaism as a race became more salient as racial and ethnic identity became the foundations for the emerging nation-state in the eighteenth and nineteenth centuries. If Jews were a race, then they could never be truly German, French, or British. This meant Jews who assimilated into modern society—even those who converted to Christianity—could still be hated because they were

165

inherently Jewish by blood, with all the attendant prejudices that Christians across Europe had imbued for centuries. And that is what happened as nationalism spread across Europe and a new anti-Semitism emerged.

Early Signs: Nationalism

Modern nationalism arose in the seventeenth century after the Thirty Years' War between Catholics and Protestants. The length and atrocities of the war led leaders and philosophers to look for ways that adherents of different religions could coexist. Nationalism emerged as a solution because it rested on people's natural connection with their native soil rather than on religion. It was accompanied by political centralization in the form of a monarch or assembly. It also had economic benefits. Thinkers such as John Locke and Erasmus saw the state as the means by which property rights could be protected, thereby paving the way for future freedoms and economic growth. Nationalism generated the feeling that states and their citizens can and should control their own destinies, and it proved to be a powerful force that inspired and then drew from the same emotional fervor and commitment as did religion.

On the surface, political nationalism seemed good for the Jews. Christianity had been the source of anti-Semitism for hundreds of years. Native soil, however, does not distinguish between different religions—and many Jews felt deep attachments to various patches of European soil. Through various expulsions, Jews had been part of the fabric of Europe for centuries. Some French synagogues were hundreds of years old. Initially, therefore, Jews greeted political nationalism with fervor—both because they were genuinely attached to their homelands and because they saw how nationalism could be a safer foundation for Jewish life than Christendom. Their enthusiasm, however, shortly waned. The events of the French Revolution show us how.

The French Revolution is a critical event in the beginning of the modern period. Beginning in 1789, it brought together a desire for political independence and national identity and a drive for equality. Old hierarchies, such as the monarchy and aristocracy, were attacked. New forms of political organization, like the national army, were created. The revolutionaries were inspired by many of the early Enlightenment thinkers, including Voltaire and Rousseau, who believed the power of human reason had been hidden by primitive structures such as the church and the aristocracy. The revolution promised a dawn of human freedom.

Yet, among the first groups targeted by revolutionaries was the Jewish community of Alsace-Lorraine, a French province. Revolutionaries attacked the Jewish community and ridiculed its backward practices and beliefs. They implemented laws forbidding the observance of the Sabbath, seeing it as a sign of difference and separation from the larger population. To be sure, Jews were not the only target of the revolutionaries, who criticized religious practice generally, including Christian practice, believing that it undermined citizens' loyalty and commitment to the state. But Jews were especially susceptible to charges of dual loyalties because they had lived apart from the larger population for so long. Their customs and even daily language differed from others in France. While Jews attained new freedoms—some Jews, though not all, were granted citizenship in France—many remained outcasts. And the aftermath of the French Revolution exposed a deep and uniquely modern source of anti-Semitism.

We can best understand that new anti-Semitism by asking an important question: why did anti-Semitism persist in the face of a promise of equality? The answer rests, in part, in lingering negative views of Jews nurtured in churches. But nationalist anti-Semitism also responded to the nature of Judaism: Judaism is not only a religion—that is, Judaism is not simply a set of beliefs and behaviors oriented toward a deity. It is not, as one philosopher described religion, "what man does with his solitude." Rather, Judaism is a way of life. It incorporates a language, a culture, a philosophy (and today, a state) alongside holidays, beliefs, and customs. The Hebrew Bible itself does not even have a word for *religion* or *Judaism* because the biblical world did not separate religion from nationality.

The modern world, however, draws exactly that distinction. We can be Baptist by religion and American by nationality. We can be French by nationality and Buddhist by religion. In the late eighteenth and early nineteenth centuries, traditional Jewish self-understanding clashed with the modern notion of religion as a private personal affair. The French Revolution brought that clash into sharp relief. Jews could not be full citizens of their country because they could not simply turn traditional Judaism into a modern type of religion. It left Jews with a difficult choice: change their ways or leave.

Here's how a French revolutionary, known as the Count Stanislas de Clermont-Tonnere, framed that choice: "It is intolerable that the Jews should become a separate political formation or class within the country. Every one of them must individually become a citizen; if they do not want this, they must inform us and we shall then be compelled to expel them."[2] The French Revolution was not an invitation to equality. It was a new, although admittedly somewhat less harsh, form of the choice that had been presented to Jews eight hundred years earlier: convert or die. The new choice offered in France and then throughout the rest of Europe was "Change your ways or leave our country." As Jonathan Sacks puts it, "the Enlightenment presented European Jews with a messianic promise and a demonic reality."[3]

Different Jews responded to this "messianic promise" and "demonic reality" differently. Some did change, abandoning traditional practices such as the dietary laws and distinctive clothing that emphasized Jewish separateness from the wider population. Some Jewish communities began praying in the native language. They promoted civic responsibility and secular learning. The Reform movement in Judaism was born in 1818 in Hamburg, Germany, as a way of adapting Judaism to modern ideals. Even so, anti-Semitism persisted. As Napoleon spread the ideals of the French Revolution across the German provinces, new taxes on Jews and residency restrictions were imposed.

One of the most dramatic illustrations of the clash between Enlightenment ideals and the anti-Semitism characteristic of nineteenth-century nationalism is known as the Dreyfus Affair.

In the 1890s, Alfred Dreyfus, the first Jewish colonel in the French army, was falsely charged with treason and stripped of his rank amid cries of "Death to the Jews." Soon after Dreyfus was imprisoned at Devil's Island, army investigators discovered the real culprit, a French soldier named Ferdinand Walsin-Esterhazy. Esterhazy had, with the aid of the chief rabbi of France, taken out a loan from a member of the Rothschild family, a famous European Jewish banking family and the focus, even today, of many conspiracies about Jewish control of the global economy. Although Esterhazy was unquestionably guilty of selling secrets to the Germans, he was acquitted and quickly fled to England.

The presence, at the edges of the Dreyfus Affair, of the Rothschilds tapped into long-standing views of rich Jews pulling the levers of the global economy, making it easier to galvanize the anti-Semites in France. But even more fundamentally, the false conviction of Dreyfus (who was eventually exonerated) dramatizes the incapacity of French nationalism to accommodate Jews to the body politic without reservation.

Anti-Semitism in Central and Eastern Europe

In central and eastern Europe, anti-Semitism persisted as well. The ideals of the Enlightenment penetrated eastern Europe more slowly, and Jews largely remained in ghettos and sectarian schools. But even there, the infectious sense of nationalism, with its double-edged impulse to both unify all inhabitants and root out those who were different, shaped areas where millions of Jews lived. While promised more rights, Jews remained outsiders. When groups of Ukrainians and Poles attacked Jewish towns, for example, local authorities did not prosecute or try to stop them. They said Jewish exploitation of local peasants and farmers justified the attacks.

These attacks—known as pogroms—were followed by more restrictive laws on Jewish movement and settlement, forbidding most Jews from settling in major urban areas under Russian control. The pogroms accelerated at the beginning of the twentieth century. Between 1903 and 1906, more than a thousand Jews were killed in more than sixty attacks on small towns across a territory occupying parts of Russia, the Ukraine, Poland, and several other countries in the Pale of Settlement.

Not coincidentally, this was a time of growing nationalism, culminating in the Russian Revolution of 1917. As in the French Revolution, the promise of quality was laudable, but the reality was familiar. Jews were quickly identified as anti-revolutionary traitors, and many fled or were murdered. By 1920, more than two million Jews had immigrated from eastern Europe to America, Britain, and Palestine.

This charge of dual loyalties followed Jews to America. Even today, questions are raised about prominent Jewish figures and their potential loyalty toward Israel. In the administration of President George W. Bush, prominent Jewish state department officials Douglas Feith and Elliott Abrams were subjects of several articles questioning their unique connection to Israel. In 2012, several prominent liberal bloggers referred to the

"Israel-firster" American Jews working for influential think tanks, even though that term had first been used by white supremacists. In 2015, radio host Diane Rehm began a question to Vermont senator Bernie Sanders—the first viable Jewish presidential candidate in a major political party— by saying, "Senator, you have dual citizenship with Israel." Senator Sanders stopped her and said that he was not a dual citizen. Rehm's producer had found his name online on a false list of members of Congress who are dual citizens of Israel. It seems to have been an honest mistake, but Rehm persisted in invoking the fake list even after Senator Sanders corrected her. The existence of the list and its use on a mainstream radio program reflect a political context in which it is acceptable to question the patriotism of American Jewish politicians. As the *Washington Post* puts it, "it's become acceptable on a wide swath of the left to question the motivations of Jews who support Israel."[4] In other words, the dual-loyalties suspicion remains a politically potent anti-Semitic tool.

A New Vocabulary for Anti-Semitism: Enlightenment Philosophy

In the eighteenth century, there were philosophical revolutions as well as political ones. This was the era known as the Enlightenment. The intellectual architects of the Enlightenment were devoted to reason and to the emerging scientific method—and many of them intensely disliked religion. Philosophers such as Kant and Voltaire said religion keeps us in a state of dependency and prevents us from figuring out truths for ourselves. It makes us moral children rather than mature adults. It perpetuates stereotypes and needless conflict.

Many of the champions of the Enlightenment believed the prejudices generated by religion could be "cured" by the embrace and application of reason. Voltaire famously said "Crush the infamy," referring to the superstitions of religion. Voltaire preferred philosophy to religion. One might think this preference would be good for the Jews. Christianity had been promoting anti-Semitism for centuries. If a more secular worldview free of religious prejudice and superstition arose, Jews would seem to have a more secure place in it. But Voltaire and other philosophes also attacked Judaism. And they saw Jews not as the victims of Christian prejudice, but as the very source of it.

Voltaire said Jews are "an ignorant and barbarous people, who have long united the most sordid avarice with the most detestable superstition."[5] He said the worst parts of Christianity are those that come from Judaism. He believed Jews' sense of group identity—the idea of being a chosen people—impeded the march of progress toward a universal humanity of shared ideas and beliefs. A truly tolerant and peaceful society depended on attaining that universal humanity, and Jews were standing in its way.

The strongest clash between the Enlightenment and Jewish tradition centered on universalism. The word itself is vague, but generally, the Enlightenment idea of universalism was one in which distinctions of dress, beliefs, and culture would fade in the wake of a power of reason, because reason arrived at certain conclusions. A certain style of artwork, for example, reflected the highest form of reason. A certain set of beliefs reflected the highest form of reason. A certain norm of dress and music came from the highest form of reason. Groups that deviated from these universal ideals were backward and primitive—and groups that excluded others on the basis of belief were backward-looking. A universalist philosophy also suggests distinctions between people made on anything other than the basis of pure reason and science are wrong. The more particular and unique a practice or tradition is, the further it strays from the ideal. The quest for a universal language— Esperanto—reflected the Enlightenment embrace of reason. And its failure to catch on showed the underlying weakness in universalism's ability to change people.

Enlightenment philosophy's commitment to universalism put Jews in a precarious position. Jews had their own set of laws and practices binding them together. Dietary restrictions and dress set Jews apart from their surrounding community. Such practices led to charges of backwardness and to accusations that Jews were clannish. Jews, so the charges went, stuck together and did not mingle properly with their fellow citizens. Johann Fichte, a German philosopher associated with the philosophical school of idealism, said the only way to make Jews civilized was to cut their Jewish heads off. The nineteenth-century philosopher Arthur Schopenhauer said Jews threaten the development of the enlightened individual and called Jews "masters of deception." He concurred with Voltaire in arguing that all the primitive parts of Christianity come from Judaism.[6] (None of these philosophers recognized that Judaism itself is universalistic philosophically. The Hebrew Bible suggests all people can achieve salvation so long as they follow a certain set of laws, the simple and short Noahide covenant. Furthermore, Judaism teaches that Israel was elected by God for the salvation of the nations of the world—Judaism, therefore, is not interested only in the well-being of Jews but in the well-being of all.)

Reading these Enlightenment philosophers feels shocking. Harsh language from such revered thinkers seems out of place. For those who love philosophy, reading philosophers' anti-Semitic vitriol may result in feelings of horror that resemble some Protestants' feelings after reading Martin Luther's comments about Jews. The words and ideas seem inconsistent with their overarching philosophies and other insights. But in fact, universalism is not just a philosophical problem. It presents a much greater danger because it can bleed into violence. As Jonathan Sacks has pointed out, "To universalize, to apply modes of thought that work for science to human beings, is to dehumanize human beings. Hence philosophy in the Platonic-Cartesian-Kantian mode is no defense against genocide. Allied to hate, it makes it possible."[7]

Eugenics

Discourses about Jews' supposedly inadequate commitment to universalism were not the only new form anti-Semitism took in the modern era. The nineteenth century also saw the rise of an anti-Semitism grounded in the eugenics movement. Eugenics sought to be the "science" of ethnicity. In the wake of Charles Darwin's work on evolution and survival of the fittest, it gained much attention and support in the nineteenth and early twentieth centuries. It looked for a scientific basis for physical and mental traits associated with a group. Scientists tried to connect body types and intelligence levels with various ethnicities. At various times, they identified different racial types, such as white European, American Indian, Black African, Asian, and a catch-all miscellaneous group called "monstrous." They assigned various traits to these groups: laziness, miserliness, craftiness.[8]

Jews were one of the most frequent targets of examination. A representative document from 1938 called "The Racial Biology of the Jews" claimed to analyze fingerprints, blood types, and susceptibility to various diseases among Jews. To this purported analysis it added the claim that Jews have "hooked noses, fleshy lips, ruddy light yellow, dull-colored skin, and kinky hair." They also have a slinking gait and a "racial scent." This was anti-Semitism disguised as science.[9]

The term *anti-Semitism* itself emerged out of the pseudoscience of eugenics. A writer named Wilhelm Marr coined it in a book he wrote called *The Way to the Victory of Germanism over Judaism*. He argued that Jewish Semites lacked within themselves the Christian-German spirit. It was simply not within their makeup, no matter how long they had lived in Germany. The Jewish spirit of intellectualism and greed was in conflict with the German folk spirit, and the Jews were winning because political emancipation had brought them into wider society. The Jews, he said, were beginning to control German finance and industry, and if the German folk did not fight back, they would die as a people.[10] Along with writing the book, Marr formed the Anti-Semitic League. It was committed exclusively to fighting the Jewish threat to German society and expelling Jews from the country.[11]

You might find it surprising that the terms *anti-Semite* and *anti-Semitism* did not arise until the late nineteenth century. As we noted earlier, hatred of Jews is one of the world's oldest and most persistent prejudices. But the word *anti-Semitism* marks a significant change because it marries religious and racial prejudice. It targets Jews not on the basis of what they believe but on who they are. Jews are not just different. They are inherently inferior.

What made this new type of anti-Semitism even more dangerous was that a "scientific" theory of anti-Semitism allowed for a "scientific" solution to it. Science is the language of cause and effect, of problem and solution. For Wilhelm Marr, the Jews were a problem that could only be solved by total assimilation or expulsion from Germany. They were immutably different from other Germans. Hitler and the Nazis took up this perspective. As we will see, they brought a technological and scientific precision to their solution to the "Jewish problem."

Intelligence, Prejudice, and Genocide

The intertwining, in the eighteenth, nineteenth, and twentieth centuries, of philosophy, science, and hatred of the Jews make clear that education and reason are not the solution to prejudice. The Enlightenment ushered in a philosophical anti-Semitism alongside racial and religious anti-Semitisms.

Its adherents envisioned a world free of prejudice while remaining blind to one they maintained. They believed the mind could solve all the prejudices lodged within our psyche. Instead, the technologies they helped create gave new powers to the ancient hatred they helped sustain. Some of the most horrific views about the Jew came from the most intelligent people.

I saw this on a visit to Germany in 1999. I was between my junior and senior years in college. A scholarship funded by the German government and a Jewish college student association allowed me to go on a three-week guided trip through Germany with fifteen other college students. I could not wait to go. I figured it would be a great way to experience Europe with peers for little money.

The trip quickly turned into a more serious and consequential experience. The most memorable part was visiting a home in a suburb outside of Berlin called Wannsee. This home was the setting for a meeting of sixteen leaders of the Nazi Party, where they drew up the plans for the "Final Solution," the array of death camps in which they planned to murder the entire Jewish people.

Driving toward the house, you would think you are in an upscale American suburb with wide lots and beautiful landscaped homes. The streets are tidy with stately trees arching over them. All the markings of culture, success, and decorum are there. You'd think this was the area where the most educated and civic-minded citizens live. And you would be right. But you would also be right in concluding that those very same people plotted the murders of millions. They did so while eating meals plated on formal china, as classical music played in the background.

I remember walking around the Wannsee home and struggling between feeling awe and admiration for the beauty of the setting and feeling horror at what went on there. I always thought education and culture promoted morality and doing the right thing. Isn't that why I had gone to Stanford and worked so hard in school, and why my parents had pushed me so hard to get a good education . . . so that I would be a good and kind person, a *mensch* (that's the Yiddish word for "a good human being")? But the people who gathered in that house and lived in that neighborhood strove for those same educational and professional achievements. They valued culture and learning. That didn't prevent them from organizing a genocide.

At that home, for the first time, the Holocaust and the horrific consequences of anti-Semitism became visceral to me. I had learned about it through both books and lectures. Now I felt an understanding in my heart. And that day, I began to understand that we cannot erase hatred with reason or by simply teaching tolerance. Thinking and learning from others is essential. Yet, a faith—a commitment to a set of values with human dignity at its core—matters more.

Around that same time I came across a quote from the great twentieth-century rabbi Abraham Joshua Heschel. It echoed this understanding and showed me why faith is so important. Heschel himself escaped Germany just before the war began. He was able to come to America and teach at a rabbinical school in Cincinnati—the same one I attended—under the Refugee

Scholars Program, which allowed seminaries to invite leading scholars to teach, bypassing normal immigration quotas. His entire family remained in Europe, including his siblings, and every one of them was murdered.

Someone asked Heschel how God could have allowed the murder of so many innocent people. He replied that the Holocaust is not a problem for God. It is a problem for human beings. It was human beings who murdered one another. It was human beings who destroyed the image of God that resides in every human being. Germany was the highly educated country in Europe in the 1930s. Yet, over 90 percent of its citizens supported Nazis by the end of the 1930s. Education did not teach people to reverence humanity.

With the best intentions, the thinkers of the modern world failed to stop a new form of anti-Semitism: dehumanization. We can even say they created it. The tools of the Enlightenment gave anti-Semites a new language and justification: Jews are subhuman. Their slave morality and superstitious faith impede the development of humanity, which is the goal of the modern world. Moreover, they are clannish. They are a cancer on society. The only way to defeat the cancer and save the patient is to eliminate the cancer. Thus, the Final Solution seemed like a logical next step in the evolution of anti-Semitism.

Hitler's Science

Scholars debate whether the Holocaust was an expression of religious anti-Semitism. Were the Nazis acting out the ultimate expression of the anti-Jewish hatred that had been taught in churches for centuries? Or was the Holocaust an expression of the modern racial, pseudoscientific anti-Semitism? By discussing it in this chapter, I am siding with the second point of view. The Nazis were secular. Yes, many of its leaders came from Christian backgrounds, as did most Germans. And yes, some churches and pastors supported the Nazis. But the Nazis revered the state and the Führer above all. Pseudoscientific racial theories were part of their party platform. The death camps were organized through rational bureaucratic procedures. They employed scientific processes and perspectives. Doctors, for example, used torture in conducting tests on blindness and in determining differences between identical twins. They documented every finding as a scientist would. Some of their papers are still consulted today. The Holocaust was not a chaotic expression of pent-up hatred. It was organized, bureaucratic, and systematic genocide. Jews were not human beings created in the image of God. They were leeches on society who could be drained for all they were worth and then eliminated. Care was taken to be as cost-efficient as possible in doing so. Even the gold fillings from murdered Jews' teeth were extracted before their bodies were cremated. Such genocide was possible only because the Nazis and their allies saw Jews as less than human. And that conception was only possible because of the history of anti-Semitism, which shrank Jews to a physically inferior, slavish people.

Another reason the Holocaust is more of a secular modern expression of anti-Semitism is captured by Yale historian Timothy Snyder. According to Snyder, Hitler saw the natural order as one of survival of the fittest. Species and ethnicities compete with one another. The strongest survive. Equality, mercy, and kindness are not part of this order. Rather, conflict is the norm. Jews, however, introduced a different kind of order. Genesis 1:26 says every human being is created in the image of God. Thus, Jews brought a notion of human dignity and equality into creation. Snyder argues that with these concepts, Jews introduced a level of abstraction to human existence. Life was not simply about fighting for your tribe's survival. It was about living according to transcendent values. For Hitler, that was unnatural. That went against the dictates of nature.

As Snyder puts it:

> What Hitler says is that abstract thought—whether it's normative or whether it's scientific—is inherently Jewish. There is in fact no way of thinking about the world, says Hitler, which allows us to see human beings as human beings. Any idea which allows us to see each other as human beings—whether it's a social contract; whether it's a legal contract; whether it's working-class solidarity; whether it's Christianity—all these ideas come from Jews.[12]

In other words, basic empathy and respect for others is unnatural. Treating others as we ourselves would want to be treated has no place in the real world. "Doing unto others"—when the "other" is a Jew or alien—allows unfit, weak species and peoples to stay alive and thereby challenge the natural dominance of the strongest. By articulating the idea that everyone equally bears God's image, Jews brought disorder and alarming instability into society

Hitler's anti-Semitism differs significantly from the traditional Christian anti-Semitism. Augustine and Martin Luther believed Jews committed the sin of murdering Jesus and thereby lost God's favor. Hitler believed Jews introduced human dignity into the world, and thereby upset natural hierarchies. To simplify it further, we could say Christians hated Jews because Jews took God (in the form of Jesus) from the world. Hitler hated Jews because they brought God (in the form of the claim that all people are created in God's image) into the world. As such, Jews are a permanent stain on the world that must be eviscerated.

How the Holocaust Helps Us Think About the Present

Thousands of books have been written detailing the horrors of the Holocaust. Our specific concern here is understanding and combating anti-Semitism in the present, and the Holocaust gives us some categories we can use in thinking about our own day.

One of the key connections between the 1930s and today is that the Holocaust was not just a crime against the Jews. The Nazis targeted Gypsies, homosexuals, the handicapped, Jehovah's Witnesses and others who did not fit the Aryan ideal. Hatred of Jews signaled hatred toward others. Anti-Semitism exemplifies dislike of the unlike. And that dislike spreads quickly.

The Holocaust also reminds us how much damage can be done on the basis of lies. During the 1920s and 1930s, lies about

Jews' greed, their hatred of Germans, and their exploitation of other people abounded. Those myths fueled the murders of six million Jews and five million other minorities.

Today, as we see a rise in anti-Semitism, we also see five new myths, all centered on the Holocaust itself. These myths try to exploit the Holocaust as a way of attacking Jews. One myth is *the Holocaust never happened*. This myth abounds in parts of the Arab world, where the Holocaust is seen as a way of legitimating Zionism and the conquest of Arab land. A second myth, pervasive in the Arab and Muslim world, is that *some parts of the Holocaust happened, but Hitler didn't finish the job*. That's now the job of Israel's enemies. A third myth is that *the Holocaust happened, and the Jews deserved it*. A fourth is that *the Holocaust happened, and now the Jews are the new Nazis who are murdering the Palestinians*. And a fifth is that *Jews get special treatment because of the Holocaust*. Yes, the argument goes, millions of Jews were murdered. But many genocides have happened in human history. Jews are exploiting public sympathy to get more money for Israel and to cover for their persecution of Palestinians.[13]

We see variations on those five Holocaust myths in the West and in the Arab world. Most of this book has considered anti-Semitism in Europe and America, but a variety of anti-Semitic tropes also flourish among Muslim communities in the Middle East. The anti-Semitism that marks Islamic communities is a relatively new phenomenon, and it is one to which we now turn.

Teesha Hadra & John Hambrick

Authors of *Black and White: Disrupting Racism One Friendship at a Time*

The point Rabbi Moffic makes is as simple as it is painful. In the centuries that gave us the Enlightenment, the US Constitution, and the French Revolution, the Jewish people should have enjoyed an unprecedented amount of freedom and acceptance. Instead, anti-Semitism flourished. As Christians, this is particularly painful to hear because the church has been complicit in or even supportive of persecution of the Jewish people. Unfortunately, the Christian church is no stranger to this kind of inconsistency in its profession of faith and its actions. In fact, the church has been used to *justify* many of those actions. A Georgia minister used Scripture as the foundation for the reorganization of the Ku Klux Klan in 1915. A somewhat infamous photo taken in the early 1900s is illustrative of this point. In the photograph are several rows of people all wearing the archetypal white robe and white pointed hood of the Ku Klux Klan. They are gathered in a church beneath a banner that spans the length of the wall. In big block letters, the banner reads "Jesus Saves."

Rabbi Moffic's work is an important reminder that

an individual's affiliation with the Christian church does not necessarily provide immunity from the possibility of committing atrocities or from standing by while others commit atrocities against our neighbors. We must instead stay alert to the prevalence of anti-Semitism, which Rabbi Moffic argues is an indicator of the health of our nation's social fabric. More important, we must ask how we can eliminate the vestiges of anti-Semitism among us today and make sure that the church will never again attack the faith from which it was born.

9

Islam, Israel, and Anti-Semitism

I n the previous chapter, we looked at new forms of anti-Semitism that emerged primarily in Europe, in more-or-less Christian countries, in the eighteenth and nineteenth centuries. In this chapter, we'll look at another form of anti-Semitism that emerged in the nineteenth century: Islamic anti-Semitism. Yes, you read correctly—Islamic anti-Semitism is not an immutable feature of world history. It is a relatively new creature, only about two hundred years old. Until the nineteenth century, Jews had more opportunities and freedoms in Muslim countries than in Christian ones. How that changed—and how we got to where we are today—is the subject of this chapter.

If you were a Jewish family in the 1400s and you could choose any place in the world to live, you would likely choose a Muslim territory. Perhaps you would choose Persia or North Africa, or the Persian Gulf or Iraq. This seems shocking today, when Jews are virtually banned from living in most Muslim countries. Yet, the sad truth is that, whereas the relationship between Jews and Christians has never been better, the relationship between Jews and Muslims has rarely been worse. Few books on anti-Semitism to date have explored the relationship between Jews and Muslims. But to ignore that story today would paint a false and distorted picture of anti-Semitism and the challenges we face.

Origins

Even though Islam is a relatively new religion by Jewish standards, having been founded in the 600s, the basis of the relationship between Jews and Muslims goes back much further, to the life of the biblical Abraham. Abraham had two sons. The first, Ishmael, was the son of Hagar, who was the servant of Abraham's wife, Sarah. The second, Isaac, was the son of Abraham and Sarah. When Isaac was born, Sarah banished Hagar and Ishmael from their home. The Bible tells a harrowing story of Hagar and Ishmael almost dying of thirst but surviving, with Ishmael becoming the progenitor of a great and mighty people. That people became the Arabs or, as the Bible calls them, the Ishmaelites.

We do not need a PhD to see that this origin story for the Jews and Arabs raises serious issues. Why did Abraham seem to reject his first son and his mother? Why did Sarah want them to leave? Did Isaac and Ishmael ever have a relationship? Did Ishmael ever have a relationship with his father?

Since Islam dominates in the Arab world, all these questions hang over the relationship between Jews and Muslims today. Even if one does not put too much credence in psychological interpretations, we know that serious Jews, Christians, and Muslims look to sacred texts for guidance, and all of our sacred texts tell this origin story. Thus, we know that the relationship between Jews and Muslims goes beyond land, war, and politics. It goes back to our origins. We are connected as family, and family conflicts can last for a long time.

Beginning of Islam

The relationship between Jews and Muslims formally began during the lifetime of Muhammad, the prophet who founded Islam. One of Muhammad's first military victories was against a group of Jews who controlled an area named Khaibar in the Arabian Peninsula. As Muhammad conquered more territory and spread the message of Islam, he argued that Jews might embrace his message as the purest form of monotheism. When this outreach failed, tensions grew. By 629, Muhammad had conquered all of the Jewish communities of the central Arabian Peninsula, and as a result of their rebuffing his outreach, Muhammad stopped instructing Muslims to turn toward Jerusalem in prayer. Rather, they should face Mecca.

Another result of Muhammad's conquest of the Jewish community was a legal idea known as *dhimmi*. The term *dhimmi* denotes non-Muslims living in Muslim countries. Laws required dhimmis to give 50 percent of their harvest to their Muslim rulers. This idea was applied in urban contexts as well and became known as the *jizya*, a tax non-Muslims under Muslim sovereignty had to pay on their produce or income because they enjoyed the protection of their Muslim rulers. But the purpose of the jizya was not just to pay for protection. The tax was meant to humiliate the dhimmis. They were infidels. Yet, infidels did have legal protections. And some rulers emphasized protections more than humiliation. As Professor Martin Gilbert points out, "During the two centuries following the death of Mohammed, Muslim rulers developed conflicting approaches towards their Jewish subjects. The difference in their approaches revealed an internal struggle within Islam, one that swung rulers between the two extremes of protection and intolerance—a struggle that has defined the Muslim-Jewish relationship to this day."[1]

This pendulum of Muslim-Jewish relations meant that in the worst of times, synagogues would be destroyed and Jews forced to convert, leave, or die. In the best times, Jews remained outside of the highest echelon of politics and culture, but they enjoyed freedom and influence. This was the case throughout Spain and Egypt for a good part of the eleventh century. Jewish culture flourished, and Jewish merchants and traders contributed immensely to economic life.

The times of destructive intolerance tended to occur when Jews were perceived as overstepping their bounds. In 1066, for example, the golden age of Jewish life in Islamic Spain came to an end when an influential Jewish leader named Samuel Ibn Negrella was, along with his son, assassinated—people had learned he'd been planning to set up a separate Jewish principality in Almeria. More than five thousand Jews were killed in the ensuing riots—that's more than were murdered during the beginning of the Crusades in Europe.

Maimonides, the greatest Jewish sage of the Middle Ages, experienced both the highs and lows of Jewish-Muslim relations. He was born in and lived in Spain until it was conquered by an extremist group from North Africa known as the Almohads. Then he fled and settled in the Moroccan town of Fez, where many scholars believe he converted to Islam in order to stay alive. Eventually he moved to Egypt and served as the physician to the sultan. His writings on the Muslim persecution of Jews are poignant and personal. In a letter to the Jews of Yemen, he wrote, "No nation has ever done more harm to Israel. None has matched it in debasing and humiliating us. None has been able to reduce us as they have." Nevertheless, as he wrote in another letter, "We have done as our sages of blessed memory instructed us, bearing the lies and absurdities of Ishmael. We listen but we remain silent." Even with his feelings of anger and sense of humiliation, Maimonides gained the support of many Muslims in Saladin's court in Egypt. He spoke and wrote in Arabic, and his death was mourned by Jew and Muslim alike.[2]

For the five hundred years after Maimonides's death, the tenor of Jewish life in Muslim territories varied depending on the inclinations of the ruler. During the Ottoman Empire, Jews flourished—in part because Muslims and Jews actually had fewer points of religious tension than did Christians and Jews. As Bernard Lewis points out, "The Muslims did not conceive or present themselves as the new and true Israel; they did not therefore feel threatened or impugned by the obstinate survival of the old Israel."[3] The idea of the new covenant replacing the old—supersessionism—did not shape Muslim-Jewish relations. That relationship ebbed and flowed on the basis of politics rather than religion.

Major Change

The nineteenth century witnessed extraordinary political shifts that reshaped the relationship between Muslims and Jews. These shifts coincided with the rise of European imperialism in the Muslim world. By the middle of the nineteenth century, almost all Muslim countries had been influenced by Western powers such as France, Germany, and England. The Europeans who settled in Muslim areas tended to be wealthier than native Arabs, and some territories were under full imperial control. Missionaries also brought Christianity into Muslim communities, creating religious tension. At the same time, Christians and Jews competed in Muslim areas for influence and closeness to traditional centers of power. The balance of power shifted constantly.

One incident from 1840 captures the dangers of this situation. In Damascus, part of modern-day Syria, the French consul, who felt the Jewish merchants were taking business from Christians he represented, convinced Muslim authorities to enter the Jewish quarter and arrest eight Jews on suspicion of having kidnapped a Catholic monk and his assistant. The Jews were accused of murdering the two and using their blood for religious rituals. As we know, the blood libel was a

ISLAM, ISRAEL, AND ANTI-SEMITISM

recurring charge in Christian Europe. It now appeared in the Middle East. And just as in Christian Europe, the blood libel turned violent: as it whipped around town, local Muslims rioted, burning down the main synagogue and destroying Torah scrolls. The eight Jews were ultimately tortured and executed.

This deadly incident fell far outside the normal course of Muslim-Jewish relations. Jews had always been second-class citizens in Muslim lands, but they had never been thought of as dangerous threats. Whereas medieval Christian writing cast Jews as possessing devilish powers and the ability to manipulate unsuspecting Christians, Muslim writings tended to describe Jews as weak and unthreatening. But this view was changing as interaction grew between the West and the Muslim world, and to the displeasure of many Muslims, the West's influence over Islamic areas was growing.

The Damascus affair signaled greater tension and violence to come. As anxiety about the West mingled with the arrival of Christian anti-Semitic stereotypes, anti-Semitism rose. As Bernard Lewis eloquently put it:

> With the changed circumstances of the era of European domination, the non-Muslim ceased to be contemptible in Muslim eyes and became dangerous. In the case of the Jews, this new attitude was further encouraged by the importation of certain ideas characteristic of European anti-Semitism, but previously unknown even to the most prejudiced Islamic opponents of Jews and other non-Muslims.[4]

In other words, Jews became a convenient victim of anti-Western sentiment.

Those shifts accelerated in the twentieth century, and they fed into the anti-Semitism we see in the Middle East today. As usual, this anti-Semitism is not just about Jews. Jews represent Western culture and globalization and the forces seeming to undermine Muslim sovereignty and values. And then there's Israel. Many Arabs see Israel as an outpost of Western culture—and West-backed power—in the Middle East. Contemporary anti-Semitism in the Muslim world is inextricable from the broader context of the creation of the state of Israel.

Zionism and Muslim Anti-Semitism

During the nineteenth century, the area that would become modern-day Israel was under the sovereignty of the Ottoman Empire. (In discussing that area pre-1948, I use the terms "Palestine" or "the British Mandate." When discussing events after the 1948 establishment of the state of Israel, I refer to both "the state of Israel" and "the Palestinian territories.") It was a relative economic and cultural backwater of the empire. Many of the Arabs who owned the land lived in larger, more developed areas, such as Baghdad and Egypt. Those living in Palestine generally worked land owned by others. The few Jews in Palestine lived in or near Jerusalem and survived on donations from Jews around the world.

The politics in western and central Europe began to affect the Arab world in the nineteenth century because of the rise of imperialism and the technologies that enabled faster travel and trade. More Europeans visited Palestine and other Arab countries, writing about their experiences and, in turn, inspiring more visits. In addition, in 1860, the first global Jewish organization—known as the Alliance Israelite Universelle—was formed in Paris. It sought to protect Jews from violence around the world. It also coincided with the rise of prominent individual Jews, such as Claude Montefiore in England, who served as global Jewish diplomats trying to look after the interests of Jews all over the world.

This global Jewish diplomacy helped fuel modern Zionism, which was the political movement to build a Jewish state in the biblical land of Israel. This is not a book about Zionism or Israel, so we cannot cover the full story. But to understand contemporary anti-Semitism, we need a quick sketch of the Zionist movement that emerged in the 1800s.

Over the centuries, since the destruction of the Temple in Jerusalem in 70 CE, Jews had prayed for but, with few exceptions, did not act in an organized way to actualize a return to Israel. They mostly followed the prophet Jeremiah's moving call to pray and work for the peace of the city where you live. Many rabbis suggested only God could restore the Jewish people to Zion—human beings should not try. In the middle of the nineteenth century, however, nationalism began to sweep Europe. While many Jews embraced, or tried to embrace, French, German, and Italian nationalism, others felt that taking on French or German identities would require wholly setting aside Jewishness or even converting to Christianity. In eastern Europe, as we have seen, Jews remained subject to residential and political isolation and to violence. The promise of a better political status and civic equality seemed far-fetched. Out of that frustration, and in the context of a world increasingly fired up by the idea of nationalism, was born the idea that Jews could create their own nationalist movement and return to their ancient homeland.

The first large group of Jews left Europe for Palestine in 1881. More followed. At first, there was little tension between the new Jewish settlers and the Palestinians—in part because Jews built communities and farms employing many Arab workers. Everyone benefited as the economy grew.

But the next wave of immigrants, in the early twentieth century, were imbued with a feeling of romantic return to the land, and they believed that Jews should be self-sufficient. Jews should farm the land. Jews should use the labor of their own hands. Increasingly, there was tension between these new Jewish settlers and the surrounding Arab populations. As we noted earlier, resentment toward Jews and Westerners had already grown with the rise of imperialism. Those tensions became more acute as Jewish immigration to Palestine accelerated in the 1920s and as the United States implemented drastic immigration restrictions, leading even more Jews to immigrate to Palestine. The Balfour Declaration of 1917 envisioning a future Jewish national homeland also led to organizational Arab opposition. It was a symbol of Western imperialism and Jewish power. In 1929, rumors that Jews were planning to take control of the Temple Mount in Jerusalem led to an outbreak of violence in the city of Hebron, leaving almost seventy Jews dead and several synagogues destroyed. Hundreds were saved by Arabs who hid Jews in their homes. The 1930s witnessed ongoing and increasing hostility as Jews left Europe, and Arabs and Jews competed for British support. That tension grew when the Islamic leader of Jerusalem (known as the Mufti) allied himself with Hitler. When the British Mandate ended in 1948, Israel declared its sovereignty.

Modern Israel

Even though the United Nations approved the creation of a Jewish state in 1947, the 1948 Declaration of Independence was met by attacks from surrounding Arab countries. The 1948 war ended with a cessation of hostility but not a formal peace. Then, in 1967, Israel defeated surrounding Arab states and gained military control over East Jerusalem, the West Bank, the Gaza Strip, and the Sinai desert. Anti-Semitism from the Muslim world grew substantially after 1967, in part because Israel now had sovereignty over millions of Arabs living in the West Bank and Gaza. The 1967 war, known afterward as the Six-Day War because of its brevity, had great psychological resonance. Israel had not only survived but had defeated Arab armies in an astoundingly short period of time. Even more than the survival of Israel after the War of Independence in 1948, the Six-Day War symbolized Jewish power.

This historic development put Jews in a relationship with Muslims almost wholly unlike the experience over the previous fourteen hundred years, in which Jews had been servile, relatively unimportant residents of Muslim lands. Now Jews held the most powerful country in the Middle East. Feelings of utter dismay and anger at Jewish might and success spread. Professor Bernard Lewis puts it in context: "The dominant note in the Arab response to [the Six-Day War] was one of shock and outrage that these defeats should have been inflicted upon them by a group of people whom they had been accustomed to stereotype as weak, cowardly, and in general contemptible—the people whom God himself had punished with abasement and humiliation."[5] Indeed, much of the vitriol of contemporary Muslim anti-Semitism stems from 1967. Hostile views of the West that began in the nineteenth century became attached to the Jews and Israelis of the twentieth and twenty-first. The frequent appearance of classical European anti-Semitic stereotypes such as the blood libel made this anti-Semitism even more toxic.

Another strand of contemporary Muslim anti-Semitism is the view of Israel as a neo-imperialist state, a continuation or extension of nineteenth-century imperialism, with Jews and Israel's other backers behaving just as their Western predecessors did. Israel not only humiliated the Arab world but also subjugated the natives of the land and prevented national liberation. In this context, the Arab League created the Palestine Liberation Organization (PLO). (It was formed in 1964 but gained prominence after the 1967 war.) The PLO sought to portray Israel as the biblical Goliath of the Middle East. The Palestinians were David, fighting the more powerful bully. This narrative gained traction in the Arab world and among some members of the political left, as we discussed in chapter 1.

All told, the creation of the modern state of Israel became

a cauldron in which a lingering, century-old resentment of Western influence mingled with new anger and humiliation—for many Muslims in the post-1948 Middle East, Israel was a toxic state, and its presumed and actual supporters the world over were the target of many Muslims' ire.

Three Anti-Semitic Claims

Today, Muslim hostility toward Jews is articulated in three primary idioms: a rejection of the legitimacy of Israel, the use of European anti-Semitic tropes such as the blood libel, and a distortion of the meaning of human rights. Not all Muslims share these views. Not all Muslim states endorse them. But anti-Semitic extremists embrace all of them.

Rejection of Israel is not merely a tactic for gaining power. Muslim rejection of the legitimacy of the state of Israel is anti-Semitic insofar as it renarrates Jews not as a people but merely as practitioners of a religion. Such a narration denudes Judaism of its essential character and tells Jews that they are not who they think they are. The Palestinian national charter reflects this point of view. As it reads, "Judaism, because it is a divine religion, is not a nationality with independent existence. Furthermore, the Jews are not one people with an independent personality because they are citizens to their states."[6] In other words, Jews are solely adherents of a religion rather than a people. If Judaism is solely a religion, rather than a nationality, then Jews have no claim to a particular land. They can live and practice their religion anywhere.

This view of Judaism is a significant distortion. Jews

began as the children of Abraham. They were a family that became a clan and then a group of twelve tribes derived from common ancestors. Religious practices exist only within this communal framework. In Judaism, belonging is more important than believing. Remember, the Hebrew Bible contains no word for *religion*. Identification with a people precedes faith and prayer.

Compare a synagogue, for example, to an Episcopal (or Presbyterian or Methodist or Catholic) church. If you were to go into the sanctuary of the church, you would find an Episcopal prayer book. But if you went into the church's kitchen, you probably wouldn't find an Episcopal cookbook. Any synagogue, however, would have both a Jewish prayer book and a Jewish cookbook. A synagogue does not just bring Jews together to pray. It encourages cooking Jewish foods, speaking Hebrew, learning Israeli dance, and doing all kinds of cultural activities as part of being Jewish. Jews are a nation and a culture, not just a religion.

Yet, Muslim theology and Arab nationalism have no room for Jewish peoplehood. Jews are a dhimmi group with religious rights but subordinate to the dominant Muslim community. They do not have any right of self-determination or self-government. They have no claim to the land of Israel because they were never a nation living there. They may have been a religious group practicing there, but never a self-governing community with a legitimate national claim. Not all Muslims think this, but it is one reason that only three Muslim-majority countries have diplomatic relationships with the state of Israel.

Blood Libel

The blood libel began as a malicious and false charge made about Jews by medieval Christians in western Europe. It appears today in television and newspapers in the Middle East. I remember a moment in 2014. It was July 28, and Israel had sent troops into the Gaza Strip in response to a kidnapping and bombardment of rockets. A spokesman for Hamas—the political group governing the Gaza Strip—appeared on CNN. I was at the gym, watching it, and almost fell off the treadmill when I heard his words. He said Israeli troops target women and children out of pure hatred and viciousness. They have become addicted to such killing, just as they were addicted to killing Christian children and using their blood. He then said we all "remember how the Jews used to slaughter Christians, in order to mix their blood in their holy matzos. This is not a figment of imagination or something taken from a film. It is a fact, acknowledged by their own books and by historical evidence. It happened everywhere, here and there."[7]

This argument comes not only from the public relations team of Hamas but also appears in more sophisticated and respected academic publications. Using less inflammatory language, a recent book published by Duke University Press and written by a professor at Rutgers University suggests Israeli troops deliberately maim but do not kill Palestinian youth. Their purpose is to debilitate them and make them totally dependent on the powerful colonial rule of the Israelis. The Israelis physically disable and experiment with Palestinian lives, says Professor Jasbir Puar. Professor Puar also says

Israel targets medical facilities and important infrastructure installments during conflict so as to inflict permanent but not deadly damage and keep Palestinians in as impoverished a condition as possible. I read this as an updated blood libel charge. It nurtures a myth about calculated, amoral Jewish violence to achieve some beneficial end. In this case, the end is control over Palestinian lives.[8]

Like the blood libel, the charge of deliberate maiming is also motivated by financial ends. The original blood libel charge in the book by Thomas of Monmouth was used to garner financial support from pilgrimages to the grave of William of Norwich, the murdered boy. Charges against the Israeli army raise money for Palestinian causes and radical anti-Israel organizations.

The 2014 mention of the blood libel is just one of many from the last fifteen years. It has become so frequent that Snopes—the website devoted to unwrapping false internet rumors—has a page dedicated to it. One of the representative claims they cite comes from a mainstream Saudi Arabian newspaper and was written by a professor at the country's flagship university, King Faysal University. It describes *hamantaschen*, the pastries Jews make and eat around the holiday of Purim. Hamantaschen are usually filled with jelly. But the professor suggests a different filling:

> During this holiday, the Jew must prepare very special pastries, the filling of which is not only costly and rare— it cannot be found at all on the local and international markets.

Unfortunately, this filling cannot be left out, or substituted with any alternative serving the same purpose. For this holiday, the Jewish people must obtain human blood so that their clerics can prepare the holiday pastries. In other words, the practice cannot be carried out as required if human blood is not spilled!!

Before I go into the details, I would like to clarify that the Jews' spilling human blood to prepare pastry for their holidays is a well-established fact, historically and legally, all throughout history. This was one of the main reasons for the persecution and exile that were their lot in Europe and Asia at various times.[9]

This charge is outrageous, but it is given credence by its clear presentation, academic source, and reputable publication. It also partakes of age-old Christian anti-Semitic falsehoods about Jews killing Christian children and using the children's blood in their religious rituals—on a subtle level, this new blood libel suggests to Christians that they were never guilty of anything wrong. They simply had to deal with Jewish treachery centuries before Muslims had to do the same.

The appearance of this charge on Snopes shows one of the ways to combat it: identify it as false. But online hate has a way of spreading and mutating into even more dangerous forms. Like the academic perversion of the blood libel charge, this claim has subtle resonances. It appeals to Christians by saying their earlier history was justified: Jewish persecution resulted from Jews' wickedness. This has direct implications for the state of Israel because the experience of Jewish persecution helped give moral legitimacy to Israel. If that moral legitimacy is called into question—if Jewish persecution was justified and necessary—Jews do not need or deserve a state. So, erasing anti-Semitism from the past means Israel has no legitimacy in the present.

It is no accident that blood libel began appearing more frequently in 2002. Only the year before, at the United Nations Conference on Racism in Durban, South Africa, Israel was identified as the worst human rights abuser in the world. And then the rash of conspiracy theories after 9/11 suggested Israel was to blame for the murders, and that its spy agency secretly communicated with Israelis who worked in the Twin Towers and told them to stay home.

This anti-Semitic conspiracy rhetoric continues to grow. It grew through the Arab Spring, through the backlash from the Arab Spring, and through each of the failed peace processes. And the rhetoric gets more acute. In describing the anti-Semitism among extremist Muslim communities, Bernard Lewis observed, "The level of hostility, and the ubiquity of its expression, are rarely equaled even in the European literature of anti-Semitism, which only at a few points reached this level of fear, hate, and prejudice. For parallels one has to look to the high Middle Ages, to the literature of the Spanish Inquisition, of the anti-Dreyfusards in France, the Black Hundreds in Russia, or the Nazis."[10]

Human Rights

Is there any cause for hope? We might think an organization such as the United Nations would help by promoting programs and resources to fight growing anti-Semitism. We might think the array of human rights groups such as Amnesty International would respond to the blood libel charge and, mindful of its dangerous history, work to stop the resurgence of anti-Semitism around the world. But we have seen the opposite reaction. Israel is viewed by many human rights groups as a shameful aggressor. And this perception matters because human rights are one of the few universal ideals in today's world. Every country is, in theory, bound to the United Nations Declaration of Human Rights. Even those who do not abide by them in practice are still committed to these ideas in principle. Human rights are the closest concept we have to a universal moral arbiter.

Therefore, when anti-Semites seek to delegitimize Israel, they use the language of human rights. Doing so broadens the appeal of anti-Semitism. As Harvard professor Daniel Goldhagen puts it, "the language of general humanitarian principles and of universal human rights is used as cover for people's true motivation—anti-Semitism—for attacking Israel and its Jews."[11] Human rights language serves as a cover for those predisposed to target Jews.

We see anti-Semites using the guise of human rights in five specific charges: racism, apartheid, ethnic cleansing, attempted genocide, and crimes against humanity. We covered racism and apartheid in chapter 1 when we went over the ways that some on the far left of the political spectrum describe Israel as an apartheid state built on the racist Law of Return. The other three connected crimes do not always present themselves in obvious ways (and sometimes certain charges against Israel stem from

205

legitimate political disagreement rather than purely religious or ethnic conflict)—nonetheless, descriptions of Israeli policy as ethnic cleansing, attempted genocide, and crimes against humanity fill the pages of Arab newspapers and propaganda. One particularly egregious trope is the description of Israelis as Nazis and Palestinians as persecuted Jews. Another is the charge that Jews poison Palestinian schools and deliberately target Palestinian civilians.[12] These charges may seem outrageous to us. But they are widely believed in many Arab countries, as numerous studies suggest.

Combating Islamic Anti-Semitism

Anti-Semitism is an extraordinarily useful political tool because it creates a scapegoat for economic and social problems. It fits into a coherent political ideology in which defeating Zionism and ridding the world of Jews is a way of improving the world. A world without Jews would be a world without financial manipulation and oppression of Muslims.

So how do we combat prejudice today? We will address anti-Semitism more generally in the next chapter. But how, in particular, do we answer the rising anti-Semitism found in extremist Muslim communities? Of course it is difficult for Americans or Europeans or Asians to shape what leaders in Iran or Turkey do. But we can shape the ways Jews and Muslims engage in our own communities.

A critical step in combating Islamic anti-Semitism is cultivating an awareness of Islamophobia—the fear of and prejudice toward Muslims. Islamophobia existed before

September 11, 2001, but we know it has grown tremendously since then. Its persistence reminds us how much Jews and Muslims share. We are both Semites—the literal definition of anti-Semitism brings together Muslims and Jews—and we are both subject to the world's hatred and scapegoating. Calling out Islamophobia may not change the minds of extremists, but it builds alliances with moderate and progressive Muslim communities and highlights our shared values. We need allies and ideals.

The second way to combat Islamic anti-Semitism is robust and sustained dialogue. This can come from shared study of sacred texts, such as the Torah and the Koran. We've done this in my community—students from my synagogue have met with students from a nearby Muslim community center to study different religious practices, and while we had some road bumps, we've been successful in building stronger ties. We've had Chanukah celebrations with families from local mosques, the most successful of which took place in people's homes. Judaism is a home-based religion—our most sacred moments happen not at synagogue, but in the home. The most valuable lessons we teach get expressed there. The Jewish sages called the home a *mikdash me'at*, a miniature temple. When we bring people into our home, we bring them into both a personal space and a sacred space, where God's presence can palpably bring us together and where people can visit and interact in a way that feels more intimate and less institutional; the home setting can transform a "program" into friendship.

A third way to diminish anti-Semitism is to partner for the good of the community, to stand up for shared values, and to support each other in times of need. I was struck by an incident in Victoria, Texas, in early 2017. A mosque burned down over a weekend. The cause of the fire was unknown, though arson was suspected. A local synagogue invited the mosque members to pray in its sanctuary until a new location for Muslim worship could be found. The local imam reported that the president of the synagogue—a doctor whom he knew professionally—stopped by his home after the mosque burned down and dropped off a set of keys to the synagogue building. We need more of this interfaith cooperation. To mix a couple of religious metaphors: the keys to the synagogue might be the keys to the kingdom.

Imam Hassan Selim

Islamic Center for Cedar Rapids

If there is anything Muslims and Jews should agree on it's this: anti-Semitism is ugly; it should not be tolerated and must be countered.

Growing up in Egypt, I had never met a Jew. I was however fortunate enough to leave Egypt for a quick visit to the United Kingdom, and there I met a Jew for the first time in my life. Since then, I never met a Jew that I didn't like. Before my short trip to the UK, friends cautioned me, jokingly at times, of eating the food my Jewish host family would offer me. What if it was poisoned, they said laughingly.

I wasn't worried that the food would be poisoned, but I was concerned; after all, I had never met a Jew before that. The food was fine, delicious in fact, but I just like food in general. But on a more serious note, what turned out to be poisonous was not the food, it was the ideas some of my friends had about Jews and Judaism. Unsatisfyingly so, for the Quran labels the Jews—and Christians and others—as People of the Book. Dhimis is the Arabic word for Jews, Christians, and other religious communities that live within the confines of Muslim majority societies. And unlike a popular and erroneous understanding of the word, it's not a derogatory or insulting designation. Looking at the other uses of the term should shed a clearer light on its meaning in the context of how Muslims view their religious neighbors. When a person dies, Arabs usually say, "So-and-so is in the Dhima of God." When a person makes a promise to protect something or someone they often say, "Such and such thing or person is in my Dhima." Finally, when someone makes a statement, to verify its authenticity and truth, they often say, "This statement of mine is true to my Dhima." Meaning the validity or invalidity of their statement is detrimental to their Dhima.

From these examples, and many others that I have not mentioned, it is clear that the term Dhima, and it's derivative Dhimi, is not in fact a derogatory term. When the Muslim legal system designated the term Dhimi to Jews, Christians, and followers of other religious traditions, it was elevating them to a place of honor and protection in the most dignifying way.

How and when, then, did we get from honor and dignity to my friends, jokingly or not, warning me that my Jewish host family would poison my food? This has been one of my priorities as a religious leader/Imam to first figure out and then reverse. The task is not an easy one, but it is possible. To get there, we ought to agree on one thing: anti-Semitism is ugly; it should not be tolerated and must be countered. Muslims must return to their tradition, must honor and dignify their Jewish brethren. They must offer them the protection by standing up for them against anti-Semitism everywhere and anywhere. We must build bridges, create friendships, and talk to, not about, each other. Perhaps then, as close friends, we can address some of the hard questions that puzzle and bother us all. For what we have in common is ever so precious than our differences.

10

George Washington's Vision

A s I write this book, anti-Semitism continues to morph and grow. In March 2018, Vladimir Putin made headlines by responding to questions about Russian interference in the 2016 American presidential elections by speculating that it might have been "the Jews." During the same week that Putin's comments made headlines, a key organizer of the left-leaning Women's March publicly stated her support for the virulent anti-Semitic leader of the Nation of Islam, minister Louis Farrakhan. She attended and Tweeted about a speech in which he described Jews as Satan and publicly thanked God for his continued leadership. Her comments and lack of condemnation of Farrakhan suggest that the progressive movement has an anti-Semitism problem. Even as we become more aware of its dangers, anti-Semitism continues to haunt the left and right of the political spectrum.

As I read these stories, I thought back to the grandmother who came to me, concerned about her Jewish grandson's future. Her visit came in September 2017, shortly after the neo-Nazi riots in Charlottesville, Virginia. She saw the mounting anti-Semitism and knew her grandson faced a potentially frightening and dangerously different future. She cried in my office and asked me repeatedly why everyone seems to hate the Jews. Her question not only challenged me; it changed me. It refocused me. It made me realize my children and I face a different world from the one I imagined when I completed seminary in 2006.

It is a world in which, as we have seen, Jews are targeted by leaders on both the far left and far right. It is a world where economic decline promotes a familiar retreat into age-old associations of Jews with greed and manipulation of the markets. It is a world where the miraculous reconciliation between Jews and Christians and the blossoming of interfaith relationships coexist with notions that Christianity is the religion of love and Judaism the religion of law. It is a world where the state of Israel attracts ire from around the world, and that ire is often expressed with anti-Semitic rhetoric and imagery. And it is a world where Jews have topped the list of victims of hate crimes in the United States for more than a decade.

Yet, despite the lingering stereotypes, relations between Jews and Christians have never been better. The state of Israel prospers economically and militarily. And 94 percent of American Jews say they are proud to be Jewish![1] With this in mind, we can empathize with the rabbi described in the following story.

Two neighbors come to their rabbi and ask him to settle their dispute. The first said a branch from the other man's tree fell on his fence. His fence collapsed, and the other man, he reasoned, should pay for it. He showed the rabbi a picture of his fallen tree. "You're right," the rabbi replied.

Then the second neighbor came in. "Rabbi," he said, "the branch that fell from my tree was a tiny branch. His old fence was falling apart already. My branch just tapped it and it collapsed. It's not my fault." He showed the rabbi a picture of the rickety fence before it collapsed. "You're right," the rabbi replied.

The rabbi's wife was in the room outside his study. She overheard the conversations with both men. Afterward she came in and said to him, "How can you say such things? You can't say they are both right." The rabbi looked at her, smiled, and said, "You're right."

We often hold conflicting points of view. And sometimes it's hard to untangle them.

I feel like that fictional rabbi when looking at contemporary anti-Semitism. On the one hand, life has never been better for the Jewish people. Jews and Christians have taken major steps toward reconciliation and enjoy deep and abiding relationships. In America, Jewish institutions and schools are thriving. Israel is succeeding economically and socially. A recent study showed that Israel is the eleventh happiest nation in the world.[2] And the number of Jews in the world has reached fourteen million for the first time since before the Holocaust.

On the other hand, in America, more Jews are victims of hate crimes than any other single group. Iran threatens Israel with nuclear annihilation. Anti-Semitic rhetoric has surged on the far left and far right around the world.

I experience this same tension within myself. I look at my two children and see how proud they are to be Jewish. They think about their faith with ease and without any worry about hate or persecution. For them, anti-Semitism is a phenomenon of the past. But then I talk to my parents, and they thank God we have Israel—"a place to go if the world goes crazy again," they say.

And then I think to myself, *They're both right.*

So, what do we do? What we do not do is turn inward and say the world hates us and will never change. What I cannot do is sit quietly and tell myself anti-Semitism is a disease that will never be cured. While we may never be able to wholly rid the world of anti-Semitism, there is plenty we can do to arrest its spread, beat it back, and preserve the freedoms and security that allow my children to feel so safe and carefree in their Jewish identities.

We can include more education in schools about anti-Semitism, the Holocaust, and Israel. We can engage in deeper and more serious interfaith dialogue. We can hold to account those who attack Israel and Jews around the world.

But that cannot be all we do. By restricting our work to these sorts of activities, we are looking at anti-Semitism through a myopic lens. We are reflecting the view that anti-Semitism is primarily a Jewish issue, something for Jews to worry about and solve through education and dialogue. In reality, anti-Semitism is a political, social, and economic issue affecting all people. Its resurgence signals deeper divisions and problems in

America and the world. "First the Jews" is not just a quotation from the apostle Paul. It is a recognition that the fate of Jews is connected to the fate of all people. How we respond to the rise of anti-Semitism will shape the future of Christians, Muslims, Jews, and so many others.

That's not just me looking into a crystal ball. That's history. Anti-Semitism diminishes in times of political stability, strong social ties, and religious diversity. For example, in much of the eleventh century, a strong and prosperous Spanish monarchy invited Jews and Muslims into powerful positions, and together, leading scholars from all three faiths helped rediscover the classical tradition of ancient Greece. Anti-Semitism diminished and Jews became some of Spain's leading and most influential inhabitants, frequently taking on Spanish names and serving in local governments. Historians now know this era as the Golden Age of Spain.

Similarly, in seventeenth-century Holland, trade brought about great wealth and coexistence of different religious groups. Dutch traders helped build the modern West. This was the era when thinkers based in Holland, such as Spinoza and Erasmus, wrote works that significantly contributed to Renaissance recovery of classical learning and to the Enlightenment. The descendants of many of the Jews who had been expelled from Spain in 1492 found their way to Holland during the seventeenth century. They lived openly as Jews and prospered in trade and the arts, and the great series of paintings by Rembrandt of several leading Jews in Holland illustrated their integration in society.

For much of its history, America has also exemplified these

conditions. The nineteenth-century America chronicled by Alexis de Tocqueville brimmed with community associations and relative political stability. Numerous, diverse, and full houses of worship dotted the landscape. Faith and freedom reinforced each other. All of these conditions—a strong civic society, political stability, thriving religious cultures—have been undermined in recent decades. Combating anti-Semitism requires strengthening each of them.

Jewish wisdom is a useful source for that strengthening. We will look at what guidance Jewish wisdom from the past and present offers us in three critical areas: politics, society, and religion.

Politics

The Bible models a healthy suspicion of leaders and ideologies. In the Book of Samuel, for example, when the Israelites demand a king, God questions their request. He asks the prophet Samuel why the Israelites want a human king when God himself is their king. When the people persist, God relents, but tells them a king will inevitably become corrupt. Of course, God was right. Politics involves human beings, and human beings are imperfect (or, to put that in the terms my Christian friends use, human beings are *fallen*). Thus, we should not imagine our political leaders or systems or ideologies will save us. How many political and social movements have floundered and failed because the people who were the hands and feet of those movements did not foresee the extremes to which their ideals would take them?

218

We will never repair all human frailties. We will never be free of prejudice or bigotry. That is why we need to be suspicious of political leaders—and that is also why politics matters. A healthy political system relies on checks and balances and stable institutions to curb our human passions and prevent us from destroying ourselves. When these institutions work, we are able to figure out ways to live more or less peacefully together. When they do not, we destroy ourselves.

Pirkei Avot, an ancient collection of rabbinic sayings and wisdom, captured this truth. In the third chapter, we read, "Rabbi Hanina, the deputy High priest used to say: Pray for the welfare of the government, for were it not that people stood in fear of it, they would swallow one another alive" (3:2). In other words, the government protects its citizens from hurting one another. At least, that's how the standard version of Pirkei Avot puts it. But there's one ancient version of the manuscript that contains a slightly different Hebrew version of this verse. Instead of a third-person account by Rabbi Hanina it appears in the first person. Rabbi Hanina says, "If we did not stand in fear of the government, we would have swallowed up each other alive." Effective politics helps us curb the worst within us. We need the limits it imposes. Without them, we would destroy ourselves.

What does this mean practically? It means respecting diversity of opinion with civility and an eye on the ultimate goal of peaceful coexistence. This respect and civility is absent from politics in the United States—even within the Jewish community. Recall the experience recounted in chapter 1 of my wife getting pushed out of a progressive Jewish conference by dozens of rioters, many of whom were Jewish, who were angry at the way her presence at the conference supported Israel. That experience was a small taste of a community taking a step toward destroying itself. Friends of mine who are Christian ministers report similar concerns—that homogenous churches can get along, more or less, but politically diverse churches find it hard to speak civilly about their differences; the options seem to be small talk or quarrels.

This book is not the place for detailed policy proposals, but two ideas—one broad and one simple—can contribute to cultivating more civil politics. The first is instituting national service. In Israel, most eighteen-year-olds serve in the army or perform national service, such as working in an impoverished community. This requirement has helped bring together people from different social, political, and religious backgrounds, including recent immigrants. While the United States does not have a draft, national service could serve a similar function, helping address the socioeconomic, geographic, and political divisions plaguing us today. Service can counter tribalism, helping us learn how to live more peacefully and civilly with (rather than eliminating, or endlessly clashing over) differences.

History suggests that shared national service reduces bigotry, including anti-Semitism. After World War II, anti-Semitism declined markedly in America. Some of that reduction stemmed from a recognition of the horror of the Holocaust. But some of the reduction came from the experiences of soldiers from different backgrounds serving together. The play and film *Biloxi Blues* tells this story beautifully. A Jewish soldier from Brooklyn serves in a division in Biloxi, Mississippi, with a range of people from different cultures, including overt anti-Semites. The relationships portrayed in the film, especially the one between a gentle Jewish soldier named Arnold Epstein and his tough sergeant, Merwin Toomey, illustrate how interaction and a shared mission can deepen ties.

My grandfather experienced this change. Before the war, he had never left Milwaukee. He received taunts as a boy and could not buy a home in the neighborhood where he hoped to live even after receiving his medical license. He then volunteered for the army and spend two years as a doctor in Europe. He cared for soldiers leaving the field after D-Day and throughout the rest of the war. That experience brought him into contact with people from all over the world. He spent two weeks with a family in the British countryside who had never met anyone Jewish before, and they became lifelong friends whom he and my grandmother visited every year.

When he came back to Milwaukee, my grandfather was able to move into the neighborhood that had once rejected him. His patients expanded from a small group of Jewish families he knew to people from all over Milwaukee. Both he and America had changed during the Second World War. Times of war can bring out the worst in us. But they can also bring us together. So, I believe, can national service.

A second, more playful, idea is that every year, political leaders from the major parties should be required to pick an issue and make an impassioned case for the views of the other side.[3] They would have to look closely and empathetically at another's point of view. The goal is not to change people's minds. The goal is to help us see one another fully and thereby craft policies that honor our differences. This idea may seem like it has nothing to do with anti-Semitism. But it can help us create communities in which people of different faiths and opinions know one another and live in relationships of mutual respect—and that respect is key to the reduction of bigotry.

A healthy political system is a precondition of a good society, but not the cornerstone of it. Rather, as Jonathan Sacks puts it, politics is "a necessary concession to reality. Politics, in the Abrahamic vision, is not the highest good . . . It is a means to an end, no more, no less. It is there to secure peace, security, safety, and law-abidingness so that we can get on with our lives, serving God in work and worship, in family and community."[4] The context in which we do that "getting on" with the rest of life "in family and community" is our surrounding civil society.

Civil Society

Civil society refers to social institutions other than the government and the family. They bind people together over shared interests, beliefs, and actions. The last thirty years has seen people's involvement in civil society shrink, as Professor Robert Putnam described in a monumental 2000 book titled *Bowling Alone*. Putnam pointed out that more people bowl than ever before, but fewer people belong to bowling leagues. He used that observation as a jumping-off point for showing that fewer people join community groups, such as school parent-teacher associations, sports leagues, Rotary Clubs, houses of worship, and other nonpolitical social groups.[5]

This decline matters because civil and religious organizations bring together people of different socioeconomic backgrounds. Unlike country clubs or school boards, they cross ethnic and economic lines. America's lawmakers have recognized their important role by exempting them from taxes. Their very existence contributes to the community. That is not to say that every last club or organization builds up society (the Klan, after all, is a club), but overall, a thriving fabric of civil organizations is good for society. People who sing in a choir, for example, have more friends and live longer.[6]

The diminishment of such institutions helps explain the upsurge in political nastiness and divisions. We used to have lots of nonpolitical institutions that brought together people of different stripes. They have lost much of their influence. Can we reverse that trend?

The question is hard to answer. Technology has changed the way we interact. The profusion of television stations and websites means we experience different sources of information and share fewer common experiences. But human beings, as Maimonides once said, are social animals. Our humanity depends on forming relationships with others, and civil society is one of the places we form those relationships.

Renewing civil society will be hard work, of course, but it's hard work we should undertake because social ties built on trust and shared concerns serve as a bulwark against anti-Semitism and other forms of bigotry. The great twentieth-century rabbi Abraham Joshua Heschel teaches us why in a remarkable story.

Heschel was actively involved in interfaith affairs, serving as a consultant to the Catholic Church during Vatican II in the

1960s. Some of his colleagues and students wondered why he spent so much time talking with leaders of other religions when the Jewish people and community needed his attention. Why was he not using his knowledge and reputation to draw more attention to critical Jewish causes?

He responded with a personal reflection. He recalled that when the Nazis came to Warsaw and captured his parents and sisters, they had no one to call. They were alone. When something happens today, he said, he can pick up the phone and call half a dozen ministers in fifteen minutes. Social and communal ties protect us all from the worst ravages of harm.

Religion

Heschel's story teaches us that religious leaders and ideas are among the best forces for combating anti-Semitism. Christianity and Islam both have a history of anti-Semitism. But they also have a history of cultivating moral literacy. Religion helps us discern right from wrong. It guides us toward seeing the image of God in every human being. And no other group or institution has the power religion does to help us create a home for God on earth.

That's one of the reasons I wrote this book. A historian can teach us about anti-Semitic incidents. A psychologist can help us see subtle expressions of prejudice. But a rabbi speaks from the tradition of *tikkun olam*, a Hebrew phrase meaning "the healing and repairing of our world." I believe our religious communities and leaders—more than the government or other organizations—can help us stop anti-Semitism.

I take inspiration from another experience in my grandfather's life. The son of a fruit peddler, he was the first in his family to go to college. When he applied in the mid 1930s, none of his preferred schools, such as Northwestern and the University of Wisconsin, accepted him. It was a time of growing anti-Semitism. His family's home was less than a mile from Marquette University, a Catholic school in downtown Milwaukee. He walked over there and dropped off an application. A few days later he received a letter of acceptance, along with an offer of a scholarship to cover the tuition. He was stunned. The one place that accepted a Jewish boy from Milwaukee was a Catholic Jesuit school.

When religious groups and leaders can make peace with one another, we find hope for society. It's no accident that when videos want to show a happy or unexpected or peaceful ending, they often show a Jewish man and a Muslim man hugging, or a Catholic priest and an imam embracing. That picture of religious harmony symbolizes broader social harmony.

But many forms of religious observance and affiliation are declining in the Western world. In Europe, many magnificent churches serve more as tourist attractions and museums than functioning houses of worship. While America remains the most religious country in the Western world, attendance at houses of worship continues to decline gradually, and the number of people who check off "none" in describing their religious affiliation has grown significantly over the last decade.[7]

Why is this dangerous? Since religion has been a central source of anti-Semitism in the past, shouldn't we celebrate its diminished influence? Some of my closest friends say that since religion has caused so much hatred and violence, we should respond to religious decline by saying, "Good riddance!" But I often remind them that the most destructive regimes in history have been secular ones. Stalinist Russia, Nazi Germany, and Pol Pot in Cambodia come to mind.

Our faith communities have fallen short of our highest values and ideals. But without a belief in a higher power, why should we defend ideas like human dignity and freedom? What is the basis of a secular morality? Even if we could find a basis, we can argue for the importance of religion on the basis of pragmatism because, as Jonathan Sacks puts it, "No secular morality today has the force to withstand the sustained onslaught of ruthless religious extremism."[8] In other words, without robust moderate and enlightened religions, far more dangerous religions will gain greater influence.

That is not just theory. We have seen the rise of extremist religious groups. They have proved, as history has shown so many times, that religious ideals bring forth sacrifice from their believers. Secularism does not. Consumerism does not. Without a foundation in faith, the culture of freedom and human dignity forged in the West will diminish.

Of course, I don't believe that Western governments should promote religion. That's not their job, and the separation between government and religion enshrined in the First Amendment helps religious groups remain vibrant and independent. But I am saying that without a strong religious foundation, we lose the power of our convictions. Those convictions can range from the left to the right side of the political spectrum. No political party has a monopoly on faith.

Rather, a sense of faith undergirds a culture of human dignity, respect for the individual, and freedom. Jews and Judaism thrive in that environment.

Washington's Dream

My hope is an echo of what President George Washington understood more than two hundred years ago. In his farewell address of 1796, he said, "And let us with caution indulge the supposition, that morality can be maintained without religion. Whatever may be conceded to the influence of refined education on minds of peculiar structure, reason and experience both forbid us to expect that National morality can prevail in exclusion of religious principle."

What is so extraordinary about this statement is the nuance and perspective with which Washington spoke. He did not say religion is the absolute foundation of morality. Nor did he question the importance of science and reason to a modern society. Rather, he said religious principles help maintain the ideals of reason and justice we so value. So, what we think undermines religion is actually sustained by it. Faith does not necessarily or even typically lead to superstition and opposition to progress, though occasionally it might. Rather, faith nurtures in individuals and groups a commitment to the ideals of tolerance and human dignity that have created a culture of freedom and progress.

It is fitting to give Washington the last word because he also established the ideals by which Jews would find a home in America largely free of the anti-Semitism of the past. In a

227

letter to the Newport Jewish Congregation in 1790, President Washington wrote:

> Happily, the Government of the United States, which gives to bigotry no sanction, to persecution no assistance, requires only that they who live under its protection should demean themselves as good citizens. . . . May the children of the stock of Abraham who dwell in this land continue to merit and enjoy the good will of the other inhabitants—while every one shall sit in safety under his own vine and fig tree and there shall be none to make him afraid.

A copy of this letter hangs in my study. Until now, even though anti-Semitism has occasionally reared its ugly head in America, Washington's vision has largely been maintained. The task of sustaining it rests in our hands.

Notes

Introduction

1. For an overview of current statistics on anti-Semitism, see the audit by the Anti-Defamation League (ADL) titled "U.S. Anti-Semitic Incidents Surged in 2016-17," available at www.adl.org/sites/default /files/documents/Anti-Semitic%20Audit%20Print_vf2.pdf.

1. Surprise

1. Steven M. Cohen, quoted in "American and Israeli Jews: Twin Portraits from Pew Research Center Surveys," Pew Research Center, January 24, 2017, www.pewforum.org/essay/american-and-israeli-jews -twin-portraits-from-pew-research-center-surveys/.

2. See the thorough 2016 study from Tel Aviv University describing college campuses as a "hotbed for antisemitism." Dina Porat, ed., "Antisemitism Worldwide 2016," Kantor Center, http://kantorcenter .tau.ac.il/sites/default/files/Doch_full_2016_230417.pdf, p. 6.

3. Karen W. Arenson, "Harvard President Sees Rise in Anti-

Semitism on Campus," *New York Times*, September 21, 2002, www
.nytimes.com/2002/09/21/us/harvard-president-sees-rise-in-anti-semi
tism-on-campus.html.

4. Arenson, "Harvard President Sees Rise in Anti-Semitism."

5. This 1975 resolution, formally titled "UN General Assembly Resolution 3379," was based on the UN's conclusion that "Zionism is a form of racism and racial discrimination."

6. Eric J. Sundquist, *Strangers in the Land: Blacks, Jews, Post-Holocaust America* (Cambridge: Harvard University Press, 2005), 109.

7. For a summary of the events on the Oberlin Campus, see Yair Rosenberg, "How Oberlin Has Repeatedly Failed to Confront Anti-Semitism on Campus," *Tablet*, May 24, 2016, www.tabletmag.com /scroll/203330/how-oberlin-has-repeatedly-failed-to-confront-anti -semitism-on-campus.

8. Bari Weiss, "I'm Glad the Dyke March Banned Jewish Stars," *New York Times*, June 27, 2017, www.nytimes.com/2017/06/27 /opinion/im-glad-the-dyke-march-banned-jewish-stars.html.

9. Gretchen Rachel Hammond, "What's the Matter with Chicago?" *Tablet*, August 21, 2017, www.tabletmag.com/scroll/243612 /whats-the-matter-with-chicago.

10. Warren Goldstein, "An Open Letter to Tutu," *Jerusalem Post*, November 3, 2010, www.jpost.com/Opinion/Op-Ed-Contributors/An -open-letter-to-Tutu.

11. Motti Friedman, "What the Media Gets Wrong About Israel," *Atlantic*, November 30, 2014, www.theatlantic.com/international /archive/2014/11/how-the-media-makes-the-israel-story/383262/.

12. Friedman, "What the Media Gets Wrong."

13. See Jennifer Medina, "Student Coalition at Stanford Confronts Allegations of Anti-Semitism," *New York Times*, April 14, 2015, www .nytimes.com/2015/04/15/us/student-coalition-at-stanford-confronts -allegations-of-anti-semitism.html?_r=0.

14. Thomas Friedman, "Campus Hypocrisy," *New York Times*, October 16, 2002, www.nytimes.com/2002/10/16/opinion/campus -hypocrisy.html.

15. Natan Sharansky, "3D Test of Anti-Semitism: Demonization, Double Standards, Delegitimization," *Jewish Political Studies Review* 16 (Fall 2004): 3–4, http://jcpa.org/article/3d-test-of-anti-semitism -demonization-double-standards-delegitimization/.

16. Laurie Goodstein, "Presbyterians Vote to Divest Holdings to Pressure Israel," *New York Times*, June 21, 2014, www.nytimes .com/2014/06/21/us/presbyterians-debating-israeli-occupation-vote -to-divest-holdings.html.

17. The study guide, *Zionism Unsettled: A Congregational Study Guide* by Walter T. Davis, is still available for purchase at online booksellers.

18. Jean-Paul Sartre, *Anti-Semite and Jew*, trans. George J. Becker (Paris: Schocken, 1948), 18–19.

2. Mainstreaming Hate

1. For United States hate-crimes statistics, see the FBI's "Hate Crime Statistics, 2016" webpage at https://ucr.fbi.gov/hate-crime/2016.

2. Quoted in Timothy Snyder, *On Tyranny: Twenty Lessons from the Twentieth Century* (New York: Tim Duggan Books, 2017), 23.

3. Ron Kampeas, "The Alt-Right Meets the Media—and Debates the Jewish Question," Jewish Telegraphic Agency website, September 11, 2016, www.jta.org/2016/09/11/news-opinion/politics/the-alt-right -emerges-joyous-into-the-light-and-then-they-argue-about-jews.

4. Kampeas, "The Alt-Right Meets the Media."

5. Bailey Smith, quoted in "Baptist Leader Claims God 'Does Not Hear the Prayer of a Jew,'" Jewish Telegraphic Agency, September 19, 1980, www.jta.org/1980/09/19/archive/aptist-leader -claims-god-does-not-hear-the-prayer-of-a-jew.

6. George Hawley, *Making Sense of the Alt-Right* (New York: Columbia University Press, 2017), 100.

7. See Hawley, *Making Sense of the Alt-Right*, 99–100.

8. See David Nirenberg, *Anti-Judaism: The Western Tradition* (New York: W. W. Norton, 2013).

9. Emma Green, "Why the Charlottesville Marchers Were Obsessed with the Jews," *Atlantic*, August 15, 2017, www.theatlantic .com/politics/archive/2017/08/nazis-racism-charlottesville/536928.

10. Erik Wemple, "Media Issue of Campaign 2016: Anti-Semitism Directed at Journalists," *Washington Post*, November 8, 2016, www .washingtonpost.com/blogs/erik-wemple/wp/2016/11/08/media -issue-of-campaign-2016-anti-semitism-directed-at-journalists/?utm _term=.9747eea19677.

11. Hawley, *Making Sense of the Alt-Right*, 141.

12. *The Campaign*, directed by Jay Roach (USA: Warner Bros, 2012).

13. Howard Kurtz, "Pat Buchanan: The Jewish Question," *Washington Post*, September 20, 1990, www.washingtonpost.com /archive/lifestyle/1990/09/20/pat-buchanan-the-jewish-question/bfc 8e956-316d-4abb-b33b-97aace0b80d0/?utm_term=.54caef0c85a4.

14. See David Mikkelson, "Absent without Leave," Snopes website, updated September 10, 2016, www.snopes.com/rumors/israel.asp.

15. See John J. Mearsheimer and Stephen M. Walt, *The Israel Lobby and U.S. Foreign Policy* (New York: Farrar, Straus and Giroux, 2008).

16. See a thorough review of the use of *The Protocols of the Elders of Zion* throughout history at Walter Laqueur, "The Many Lives of the 'Protocols of the Elders of Zion,'" *Mosaic*, December 4, 2017, https://mosaicmagazine.com/essay/2017/12/the-many-lives-of-the -protocols-of-the-elders-of-zion/.

17. Yair Rosenberg, "Richard Spencer Says He Just Wants 'White Zionism,'" *Tablet*, August 18, 2017, www.tabletmag.com

/scroll/243556/richard-spencer-says-he-just-wants-white-zionism-heres-why-thats-malicious-nonsense.

18. Josh Nathan-Kazis, " 'Alt Right' Leader Ties White Supremacy to Zionism—Leaves Rabbi Speechless," *Forward*, December 7, 2016, https://forward.com/news/356336/alt-right-leader-ties-white-supremacy-to-zionism-leaves-rabbi-speechless/.

19. The Declaration of the Establishment of the State of Israel, May 14, 1948, Israel Ministry of Foreign Affairs website, www.mfa.gov.il/mfa/foreignpolicy/peace/guide/pages/declaration%20of%20establishment%20of%20state%20of%20israel.aspx.

20. Mark Oppenheimer, "The Specifically Jewy Perviness of Harvey Weinstein," *Tablet*, October 9, 2017, www.tabletmag.com/scroll/246724/the-specifically-jewy-perviness-of-harvey-weinstein.

21. Quoted in Sam Kestenbaum, "Anti-Semitic 'Alt-Right' Pounces on Harvey Weinstein Scandal to Bolster Conspiracy Theories," *Forward*, October 20, 2017, https://forward.com/news/384669/anti-semitic-alt-right-pounces-on-harvey-weinstein-scandal-to-bolster-consp/.

22. Anav Silverman, "Jews Less than 0.2% of World Population," Jewish Press website, September 20, 2012, www.jewishpress.com/news/jewish-news/jews-less-than-0-2-of-world-population/2012/09/20/.

23. Milton Himmelfarb, in David Zvi Kalman, "China Dolls," *Tablet*, December 8, 2015, www.tabletmag.com/jewish-life-and-religion/195557/china-dolls.

24. Zubin Jelveh, "Blaming Jews for the Financial Crisis," *New Republic*, May 19, 2009, https://newrepublic.com/article/49657/blaming-jews-the-financial-crisis.

25. "Rush Limbaugh Wonders If 'Jewish Bankers' Will Have Buyers Remorse," *Huffington Post*, updated December 6, 2017, www.huffingtonpost.com/2010/01/22/rush-limbaugh-wonders-if_n_433583.html.

26. Marc Lee Raphael, *Abba Hillel Silver: A Profile in American Judaism* (New York: Holmes and Meier, 1989), xix.

27. See Gary A. Tobin and Sid Groeneman, "Anti-Semitic Beliefs in the United States," Institute for Jewish & Community Research website, 2003, www.jewishresearch.org/PDFs/A_S_Report_web.pdf.

28. See the report, "ADL Report: White Supremacist Murders More Than Doubled in 2017," Anti-Defamation League website, January 17, 2018, www.adl.org/news/press-releases/adl-report-white-supremacist-murders-more-than-doubled-in-2017.

3. An Optimist Faces Reality

1. Gertrude Kolmar, *My Gaze Is Turned Inward: Letters, 1938–1943* (Evanston, IL: Northwestern University Press, 2004).

2. See "A Portrait of Jewish Americans," Pew Research Center website, October 1, 2013, www.pewforum.org/2013/10/01/jewish-american-beliefs-attitudes-culture-survey/.

3. Quoted in Jonathan Sacks, "Without Walls," The Office of Rabbi Sacks website, June 21, 2008, http://rabbisacks.org/covenant-conversation-5768-shelach-lecha-without-walls/.

4. Pew Research, "Portrait of Jewish Americans."

5. Paula Yablansky, "Confronting Anti-Semitism," *Interfaith Family*, May 2002, https://interfaithfamily.com/news_and_opinion/synagogues_and_the_jewish_community/confronting_anti-semitism_if_i_dont_respond_who_will/.

6. Pew Research, "Portrait of Jewish Americans."

7. Quoted in Dennis Prager and Joseph Telushkin, *Why the Jews? The Reason for Antisemitism* (New York: Simon & Schuster, 2007), 14.

8. Niemöller spoke several versions of the poem. It was transmitted orally and later written down. For a scholarly exploration of its origins, see Harold Marcuse, "Martin Niemöller's Famous Quotation: 'First They Came for the Communists . . . ,' " UC Santa Barbara, updated February 1, 2018, www.history.ucsb.edu/faculty/marcuse/niem.htm.

4. The World's Oldest Hatred

1. David Nirenberg, *Anti-Judaism: The Western Tradition* (New York: W. W. Norton, 2013).

2. Spencer Blakeslee, *The Death of American Antisemitism* (Westport, CT: Greenwood, 2000), 13.

3. Jonathan Sacks, *A Letter in the Scroll* (New York: Free Press, 2000), 93.

4. See Louis Feldman, ed., *Jew and Gentile in the Ancient World* (Princeton: Princeton University Press, 1996), 159.

5. Philostratus, *Vita Apollonii*, Loeb Classical Library series (Cambridge: Harvard University Press, n.d.), 1:541.

6. Nirenberg, *Anti-Judaism*, 22.

7. Quoted in David Wolpe, "The Changing Face of Anti-Semitism," *Los Angeles Review of Books*, December 21, 2015, https://lareviewof books.org/article/changing-face-antisemitism.

5. The Devil and the Jews

1. See "A Portrait of Jewish Americans" Pew Research Center website, October 1, 2013, www.pewforum.org/2013/10/01/jewish -american-beliefs-attitudes-culture-survey/.

2. "ADL Poll: Anti-Semitic Attitudes in America Decline 3 Percent," Anti-Defamation League, October 28, 2013, www.adl.org /news/press-releases/adl-poll-anti-semitic-attitudes-in-america-decline -3-percent.

3. See James Carroll, *Christ Actually* (New York: Penguin, 2015), 56.

4. Leon Poliakov, *The History of Anti-Semitism: From the Time of Christ to the Court Jews* (Philadelphia: University of Pennsylvania Press, 2003), 41, 56.

5. Poliakov, *History of Anti-Semitism*, 48.

6. "That Dear Old Oak in Georgia," *Economist*, December 16, 2015, www.economist.com/news/christmas-specials/21683972-long-afterlife-americas-only-anti-semitic-lynching-dear-old-oak-georgia.

7. John Chrysostom, quoted in Barry E. Horner, *Future Israel: Why Christian Anti-Judaism Must Be Challenged* (Nashville: B&H Academic), 21; and Susanna Drake, *Slandering the Jew: Sexuality and Difference in Early Christian Texts* (Philadelphia: University of Pennsylvania Press, 2013), 93.

8. Bernard Starr, "Five Stages of Anti-Semitism in Art," *HuffPost: The Blog*, February 19, 2015, www.huffingtonpost.com/bernard-starr/five-stages-of-anti-semit_b_6707728.html.

9. Starr, "Five Stages."

10. See Walter Lacqueur, *The Changing Face of Anti-Semitism* (Oxford: Oxford University Press, 2008).

11. Jeremy Cohen, *Christ Killers: Jews and the Passion from the Bible to the Big Screen* (Oxford: Oxford University Press, 2007), 106.

12. Cohen, *Christ Killers*, 109.

13. Nathan Burstein, "Mexican Town Celebrates Easter with 'Burning of the Jews,'" *Times of Israel*, April 10, 2012, www.timesofisrael.com/mexican-town-celebrates-easter-with-burning-of-the-jews/.

14. René Girard, The Scapegoat, trans. Yvonne Freccero (Baltimore: Johns Hopkins University Press, 1989).

15. Lyndal Roper, *Martin Luther: Renegade and Prophet* (New York: Random House, 2016), 383.

16. Martin Luther, *On the Jews and Their Lies*, vol. 47 of Luther's Works; trans. Martin H. Bertram (Philadelphia: Fortress, 1971), 268–71.

17. Dennis Prager and Joseph Telushkin, *Why the Jews? The Reason for Antisemitism* (New York: Simon & Schuster, 2007).

6. Is Christianity Still Anti-Semitic?

1. Jesse Eisinger, "Why the SEC Won't Hunt the Big Dogs," ProPublica website, October 26, 2011, www.propublica.org/article /why-the-sec-wont-hunt-big-dogs.

2. Timothy Geithner, *Stress Test: Reflections on Financial Crises* (New York: Broadway Books, 2015).

3. Paul Nehlen, a former candidate for Congress, recently used *Talmudic* as an insult as part of a series of anti-Semitic Tweets. See Emma Green, "Paul Nehlen Is an Anti-Semitic Clown," *Atlantic*, January 24, 2018, www.theatlantic.com/politics/archive/2018/01 /paul-nehlen/551312/.

4. Bernard Starr, "Can a Film Succeed Where Words Alone Have Failed to Convince Naysayers That Jesus Lived and Died a Dedicated Jew?" HuffPost: The Blog, October 10, 2017, www.huffingtonpost .com/entry/can-a-film-succeed-where-words-alone-have-failed-to _us_59d1628ce4b0f3c468060fd1.

5. Bernard Starr, "Five Stages of Anti-Semitism in Art," HuffPost: The Blog, February 19, 2015, www.huffingtonpost.com/bernard-starr /five-stages-of-anti-semit_b_6707728.html.

7. "He Jewed Me Down"

1. See Josh Marshall, "Trump Rolls Out Anti-Semitic Closing Ad," *Talking Points Memo website*, November 5, 2016, https://talking pointsmemo.com/edblog/trump-rolls-out-anti-semitic-closing-ad.

2. Abraham Foxman, *Jews and Money: The Story of a Stereotype* (New York: Palgrave Macmillan, 2010), 33.

3. Foxman, *Jews and Money*, 36.

4. Foxman, *Jews and Money*, 13–42.

5. "Madoff Scam Spurs Online Anti-Semitism," *Jerusalem Post*, December 20, 2008, www.jpost.com/Jewish-World/Jewish-News /Madoff-scam-spurs-online-anti-Semitism.

6. See, for example, Cecil Roth and I. H. Levine, eds., *The Dark Ages: Jews in Christian Europe, 711–1096* (New Brunswick, NJ: Rutgers University Press, 1966); and Joseph Shatzmiller, *Shylock Reconsidered: Jews, Money-Lending, and Medieval Society* (Los Angeles: University of California Press, 1990).

7. "Jewish History Sourcebook: The Black Death and the Jews 1348-1349 CE," Fordham University, accessed April 12, 2018, https://sourcebooks.fordham.edu/jewish/1348-jewsblackdeath.asp.

8. Thomas Hobbes, *Leviathan Part I* (CreateSpace, 2015), 137.

9. See Thomas Sowell, "Are Jews Generic?" in *Black Rednecks and White Liberals* (New York: Encounter, 2005), 65–110.

10. Sowell, "Are Jews Generic?" 70.

11. See Melanie Long, "Merchantry, Usury, Villainy: Capitalism and the Threat to Community Integrity in *The Merchant of Venice*," *Anthropoetics* 17, no. 2 (Spring 2012): http://anthropoetics.ucla.edu/ap1702/1702long/.

12. Long, "Merchantry, Usury, Villainy."

13. Jason Maoz, "Remembering Milton Himmelfarb," Jewish Press website, January 18, 2006, www.jewishpress.com/indepth/media-monitor/remembering-milton-himmelfarb/2006/01/18/.

8. "A Messianic Promise and a Demonic Reality"

1. Dovid Markel, "On the Origins of the Chassidic Movement," Neirot website, accessed April 12, 2018, www.neirot.com/wp-content/uploads/2015/09/On-the-Origins-of-the-Chassidic-Movement-%E2%80%93-A-Critique.pdf.

2. Quoted in Jonathan Sacks, "Love, Hate, and Jewish Identity," *First Things*, November 1997, www.firstthings.com/article/1997/11/003-love-hate-and-jewish-identity.

3. Sacks, "Love, Hate, and Jewish Identity."

4. See David Bernstein, "Why Did Diane Rehm Fall for an Anti-Semitic Hoax?" *Washington Post*, June 11, 2015, www.washington post.com/news/volokh-conspiracy/wp/2015/06/11/why-did-diane-rehm-fall-for-an-anti-semitic-hoax/?utm_term=.5ae2267a2300.

5. Voltaire, "Jews," in *A Philosophical Dictionary* (1903), 10:284.

6. See Michael Mack, *German Idealism and the Jew* (Chicago: University of Chicago Press, 2003), 6.

7. Jonathan Sacks, *The Great Partnership* (New York: Schocken, 2012), 88.

8. See Milton Kleg, "Anti-Semitism: Background to the Holocaust," Social Studies website, accessed April 12, 2018, www.social studies.org/sites/default/files/publications/se/5906/590605.html.

9. John Glad, "History, Eugenics and the Jews," Jewish Press website, June 9, 2004, www.jewishpress.com/indepth/opinions/history-eugenics-and-the-jews/2004/06/09/2/?print.

10. See Moshe Zimmerman, *Wilhelm Marr: The Patriarch of Anti-Semitism* (New York: Oxford University Press, 1986).

11. The story of the League is told in Zimmerman, *Wilhelm Marr*.

12. Timothy Snyder, "Understanding Hitler's Anti-Semitism," *Atlantic*, September 9, 2015, www.theatlantic.com/international/archive/2015/09/hitler-holocaust-anti-Semitism-timothy-snyder/404260/.

13. Jonathan Sacks outlines these myths in "Why We All Need Holocaust Memorial Day," The Office of Rabbi Sacks website, January 27, 2015, http://rabbisacks.org/need-holocaust-memorial-day/.

9. Islam, Israel, and Anti-Semitism

1. Martin Gilbert, *In Ishmael's House* (New Haven: Yale University Press, 2010), 27.

2. See "Maimonides' Epistle to the Jews of Yemen," in Norman A. Stillman, *The Jews of Arab Lands: History and Source Book* (Philadelphia: Jewish Publication Society, 1998).

3. Bernard Lewis, *Semites and Anti-Semites* (New York: W. W. Norton, 1998), 118.

4. Lewis, *Semites and Anti-Semites*, 126.

5. Lewis, *Semites and Anti-Semites*, 185.

6. See Joel Peters, ed., *The Routledge Handbook on the Israeli-Palestinian Conflict* (New York: Routledge, 2015), 394.

7. A summary of the interview and quotes is found on CNN's Belief Blog. See Candida Moss and Joel Baden, "Blood Libel: the Myth That Fuels Antisemitism," *Belief Blog*, August 6, 2014, http://religion.blogs.cnn.com/2014/08/06/blood-libel-the-short-history-of-a-dangerous-myth/.

8. Jasbir Puar, *The Right to Maim* (Durham: Duke University Press, 2017).

9. See David Mikkelson, "Jews Blood Rumor," Snopes website, updated July 13, 2007, www.snopes.com/religion/blood.asp.

10. Lewis, *Semites and Anti-Semites*, 195.

11. Daniel Goldhagen, *The Devil That Never Dies* (New York: Hachette, 2013), 79.

12. See Jonathan Sacks, "Future Tense—the New Anti-Semitism," The Office of Rabbi Sacks website, November 1, 2007, http://rabbisacks.org/future-tense-the-new-antisemitism-what-is-it-how-do-we-deal-with-it-published-in-the-jewish-chronicle/.

10. George Washington's Vision

1. "A Portrait of Jewish Americans," Pew Research Center website, October 1, 2013, www.pewforum.org/2013/10/01/jewish-american-beliefs-attitudes-culture-survey/.

2. John F. Helliwell, Richard Layard, and Jeffrey D. Sachs, eds., "World Happiness Report 2018" (New York: Sustainable Development Solutions Network), figure 2.2, https://s3.amazonaws.com/happiness -report/2018/WHR_web.pdf.

3. I first encountered this idea in a speech from Rabbi David Wolpe.

4. Jonathan Sacks, *The Great Partnership* (New York: Schocken, 2012), 132.

5. Robert Putnam, *Bowling Alone* (New York: Simon and Schuster, 2000).

6. See Kathy Alexander, "5 Benefits of Joining a Choir Backed by Science," *Voice Council* magazine, July 1, 2017, www.voicecouncil .com/benefits-of-joining-choir-health-wellbeing-russell-scott/.

7. For religious life in America, see Michael Lipka, "Why America's Nones Left Religion Behind" Pew Research Center website, August 24, 2016, www.pewresearch.org/fact-tank/2016/08/24 /why-americas-nones-left-religion-behind/. For religious life in Europe, see Naftali Bendavid, "Europe's Empty Churches Go on Sale," *Wall Street Journal*, January 2, 2015, www.wsj.com/articles/europes-empty -churches-go-on-sale-1420245359.

8. Sacks, *Great Partnership*, 109.

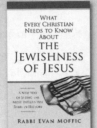

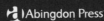